Best Practices In Investor Relations

- M. S. Anand

Institutional investors are the biggies on the block. These include the Foreign Institutional Investors (FIIs), Domestic Mutual Funds (DMFs), Portfolio Managers, Insurance Companies, Investment Bankers, Commercial Trusts, and Hedge Funds. The Institutional Investors account for more than half of the volume of trades on any of the bourses - be it domestic or international.

The money at disposal of the Institutional Investors does not actually belong to them, but it pertains to that of the general public through whom they had raised through various schemes. However, the Institutional Investors are widely influential on the stock markets as they have the capability to move large block of shares.

This Book highlights some of the Best Practices in Investor Relations (IR) which can add value to Companies that are here to stay.

Best Practices In Investor Relations

M. S. Anand

VISHWAKARMA
PUBLICATIONS
VP®

Best Practices In Investor Relations

Edition - September 2015
© **M. S. Anand**

ISBN 978-93-83572-54-0

Published by:
Vishwakarma Publications
283, Budhwar Peth, Near City Post,
Pune- 411 002.
Phone No: (020) 20261157 / 24448989
Email: info@vpindia.co.in
Website: www.vpindia.co.in

Cover Design
Meghnad Deodhar

Typeset and Layout
Gold Fish Graphics, Pune.

Printed at
Repro India Limited, Mumbai

Foreword

At no time in recent history have executives faced challenges as they have since the changing markets and the global economic crisis which unfolded dramatically in 2008. This Book brings forth the practices in Investor Relations (IR) being followed by today's managers and professionals in order to stay competitive in a fast moving world.

In their own words, prominent executives share their insights on cutting edge issues and timeless topics. Combined, these interviews create perhaps the most stimulating publication on the latest thinking in investor relations, governance, and enterprise risk management.

Since many professionals, being busy with the day-to-day job demands, don't find time to upgrade their skill set. IR Society has come forward with what's known as Continuing Professional Development (CPD), so that Professionals can devote for their own career development and personal brand building. This apart the Society also runs the regular Certification In Investor Relations too. Fast, punchy and prescient, these insights followed by interviews with industry experts by Anand M S in this book are worth book marking today for greater job enrichment, value and recognition for a better tomorrow. The book gathers together separate but related articles on IR, governance, and enterprise risk management. Besides it also contains IR Survey Results on BSE-500 companies.

We trust readers will find this book to be a valuable resource on investor relations best practices.

Sincerely,

George Chako, Consultant London

IR Survey

Over the last 2 years, we had carried out a survey with about 300-odd companies with wide variety of market capitalizations. We had requested these companies to participate in our study and among these about 45%, or 135 companies have agreed. The participants were sent a copy of the questionnaire, which they readily answered and mailed back.

It has also been found that the price volatility surrounding the earnings is of a short-term in nature and is of interest only to the momentum investors. The IR Professionals must try to build relations with institutions with longer-term investment horizons. Those investors who believe in Growth at Reasonable Price (GARP) or Value Investing styles base their decision on fundamental analysis of the company and are inclined to pick up shares of the company at lower levels.

It has also been observed that it is not very important to keep on emphasizing on growth strategy. The management's commitment and conviction is more important, especially during the downturn. The GARP or Value Investors, for instance, prefer to pick up stocks of those companies which have slower growth.

The survey findings will appear throughout the book.

Table of Contents

Investor Relations

What is Investor Relations?

Investor Relations comprises ongoing activities that companies undertake to communicate with their present and prospective investors. Companies adopt a mix of regulatory and voluntary activities during the course of their interaction with existing shareholders, potential investors, analysts and media.

Meetings with investors, presentations, media releases, website information, and annual reports are some of the segments of Investor Relations activities that are aimed to empower the stakeholders so that they can gain a greater understanding of the company's business, financial performance and the way forward.

Investor Relations is definitely not just one-way, it is in fact a dialogue which constitute queries and feedback from the investment community as well. For several listed companies, the dialogue will begin in the pre-IPO phase, when the company is profiling itself to its potential investors. Post-IPO the communication must of course continue and must be seen as a long-term, ongoing responsibility rather than an activity that is undertaken when there is a fund-raising in the offing.

With about 6000 companies listed on Asia's oldest and prestigious stock exchange-BSE and a little less on the tech-savvy-NSE, the competition for investor, analyst and media attention is very strong, and not many can afford low visibility from the investment community.

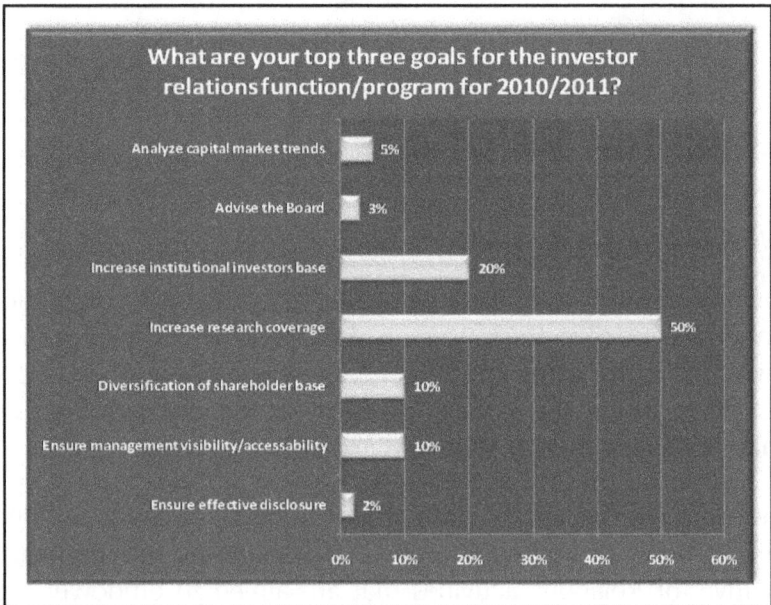

What are your top three goals for the investor relations function/program for 2010/2011?

Goal	Percentage
Analyze capital market trends	5%
Advise the Board	3%
Increase institutional investors base	20%
Increase research coverage	50%
Diversification of shareholder base	10%
Ensure management visibility/accessability	10%
Ensure effective disclosure	2%

Why Investor Relations?

"IR Leads to Fair Valuation of Equity Shares."

- Ghanshyam Dass, Sr.Advisor, NASDAQOMX and KPMG

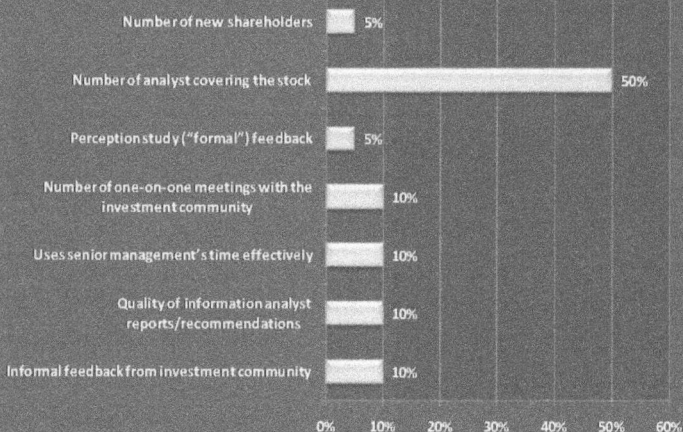

How is investor relations effective measured at your company?

Category	Percentage
Number of new shareholders	5%
Number of analyst covering the stock	50%
Perception study ("formal") feedback	5%
Number of one-on-one meetings with the investment community	10%
Uses senior management's time effectively	10%
Quality of information analyst reports/recommendations	10%
Informal feedback from investment community	10%

Besides empowering investors about your company and gaining visibility, Investor Relations also helps listed companies in gaining access to capital, achieving liquidity, and a fair valuation for their equity shares.

Access to capital

Building relationships with the investment community over a period of time so that they become cognizant with the company's investment proposition, thereby achieving an efficient and cost-effective access to capital, which is the main objective of IR. The success or failure of an IR program is judged not just by the company's ability to raise capital but also the ease with which the capital is raised.

Liquidity

Liquidity is important for institutional trades as they buy and sell in huge volumes. If the floating stock of a company is very less, then the IR program may not be successful as, generally, the IR professionals' network with institutional investors only, hence it is important to attract liquidity and maintain adequate floating stock.

Fair valuation

The end-objective of IR for a company is to achieve a fair market valuation, which is achieved by effectively managing expectations of investors. Communicating with the investment community will enable a company to detail its own record of performance and its corporate strategy. It's the duty of an IR professional to understand how his company is being evaluated and whether the market's expectation is in line with its own expectation or not.

Getting the balance right

Practicing investor relations will not automatically guarantee a company heightened profile, unless the shareholder base is properly balanced between institutional investors and retail investors. This can be achieved by updating those who already follow / know the equity story and by creating awareness to new sets of audiences.

Overall, readily available information creates insight that helps analysts and investors make informed decisions about the fundamental strengths / weaknesses and prospects of companies.

IR Builds Image in Marketplace:

Since IR highlights the benefits of using a proactive approach in disseminating vital information, it essentially becomes a marketing and brand building exercise in the marketplace. IR can also be termed as a marketing function because it is solely responsible for the shareholder mix of a company. IR can influence the decisions of investors by the information that they communicate. Decisions such as buy, hold, and sell, can be influenced with the help of a proactive IR.

Proactive IR can ensure an ideal mix of shareholders ranging from income investors and value investors to that of the momentum investors. The moment it is known that the company is moving from growth to value stock, the IR Professional will be in a position to anticipate those who shall sell and those who will be more than willing to make fresh investments.

It all depends on maintaining relationships and constantly updating the investors who matter. Even during the hour of crisis, proactive IR can stop investors from resorting to panic selling. Showcasing how strong the company's fundamentals are and explaining on the company's strategies are one of the several ways and means to give a presentation on the company's progress before the investors press the panic button.

Sponsored Research Is In Vogue

"Sponsored research widens the range of opportunities available to investors who are not able to meet the management."

- Ashish Chouhan, MD, Bombay Stock Exchange

In the small-cap and mid-cap pace, an area comprising a large number of companies which are not always widely researched, we regularly use paid-for research reports (research reports commissioned and paid for by quoted companies and procured from independent equity research providers) to support institutional decision-making process.

Some companies also find such reports useful to initiate their own research process as it means they have more information about the industry and their peers too. Indeed such research may add value for it has a third-party opinion to support investment decisions.

The availability of paid-for research, often referred to as company sponsored research, has the potential to bring a greater number of active participants in the stock trading of a company. It may be easier to raise new capital and increase liquidity of the shares already in existence if a broader base of potential investors is familiar with a company.

Reducing the liquidity risk premium should be reflected in a more favorable share price. Additionally, improved liquidity is a factor which improves the likelihood that a larger number of fund managers may consider the company. The time taken to liquidate fund holdings is an important consideration for managers of open-ended funds, who may need to sell assets to fund redemptions and cannot afford to have large positions which may be difficult to sell.

Paid-for research also widens the range of opportunities available to investors who are not able to meet the management of companies being considered for purchase. While institutional investors are able to gain access to the management of such companies and possibly spend time with them, not everyone has this opportunity. With a large universe of quoted companies, it is difficult to meet every company even if you do have access.

It is sometimes difficult to ascertain whether the research provided is sufficiently objective. We have however found that research companies are keen to develop a reputation for quality and this has been expressed by the researchers. As a result, paid-for research companies' opinions are taken more seriously because they are willing to be critical of the companies they research.

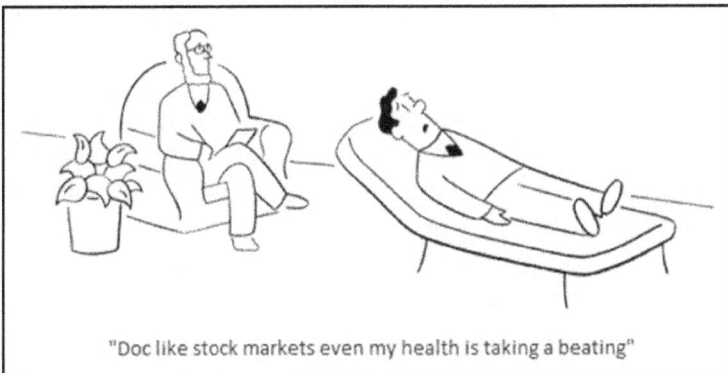

"Doc like stock markets even my health is taking a beating"

Art of managing expectations:

Since a well-informed market is likely to price the stock closer to its fair value, the skill to manage to expectations is gaining significance. This does not mean that the IR Professionals have to network only with buy-side analysts, they shall have to build relationships with the sell-side analysts as well.

Several fund managers pay greater attention to anticipated earnings results and many of their investment models solely rely on earnings expectations, hence the IR Professionals shall have to keep a close watch on the analysts' consensus forecast. Even if the quarterly earnings are far better than the corresponding quarter of last year (or that of the immediate last quarter), the share price of the company may still get battered if the quarterly earnings are far less than the consensus forecast of the analysts.

Market often reacts to the earnings forecasts. Some companies believe in giving surprises by deliberately giving conservative estimates. But this trend can raise questions as to whether the future of the company is out of the management control. This apart, if a company too frequently surprises the analysts on the positive side, analysts will soon see through the game and start pegging higher expectations.

Since last two years, the role of Investor Relations has changed considerably in the Indian context, thanks to the advent of Institutional Investors (be it in the form of domestic mutual funds, FIs, or even the FIIs).

By talking to several corporate clients, it was possible to develop an in-depth survey for finding out as to how the role of IR Professionals (IRPs) has changed.

IR Professionals May Influence Research Coverage

"Nothing wrong to expect IR professionals to influence research coverage"

- Kevin D'souza, CFO, Bajaj Finserv

NOTHING WRONG if Management expects the IR Professional to influence research coverage. The IR professional essentially connects the management and the high value investors in order to attract them to usher in the desired capital into the company. In this process, the IR professional interacts with the analysts, who present the data or their independent reports before the investors. The manner in which the IR professional presents the information before the analysts is certainly important. While the IR professional is required to provide the factual information, his way of communication can certainly influence the research coverage of analysts.

The IR Professional acts as a link between the company and its investors. In such a case, knowing the needs of its investors is important for the IR Professional. The group of investors, their objective of investment and their understanding of the company's intrinsic value are few factors the IR professional has to bear in mind while interacting with the investors.

The Investors bring in the required capital for the company and look for returns on their investments. It is therefore important for the IR professional to bring in harmony with investors.

Only when he knows the investors well, can he advise the company on various capital raising plans & corporate action matters.

Traits of an Investor Relations Professional

IR is a multi disciplinary function. An IRP must have adequate knowledge in the areas of finance, investment analysis, communications, operations, and strategic planning. Host of qualities such as being goal driven, confident, and energetic, are also required for undertaking IR function so that they can meet the demands of analysts and various fund managers.

Constant interaction with management to decide on the kind of information that needs to be disseminated, profile of investors with whom the management needs to interact on a one-on-one basis, doing perception audit as to what the institutional investors think about the management style of functioning, are some of the IR areas that call for tremendous amount of energies.

To specialize in IR, there is no tailor-made program. It generally requires people from diverse backgrounds, combining education (in finance), job experience (in finance/business journalism/financial communication) and talent (inter-personal and networking skills). Hence any person who has a broad understanding of finance, operations, and the company's overall strategy, would excel in IR.

Some of the capabilities that an IR person is normally required to have includes:

1. Practical knowledge on capital markets and investor behavior. This is normally acquired only through constant interaction with analysts/portfolio managers and making presentations on behalf of the company

2. Broad understanding of technology used for disseminating vital information to analysts/portfolio managers/investors. Technology requirement includes holding webcast, conference calls, and others.

3. Comprehensive understanding of financial structure of the company is mandatory. An IR person should be able to interpret the balance sheet and do number crunching which will come in handy while interacting with analysts. A few others tend to get into IR through the communications background, while some enter IR through the operations route. The Thapar group company, Ballarpur Papers, for instance, had an IR person who was an engineer by profession and had spent a considerable amount of time in the company in the operations department.

4. Should have an eye for 'unfolding news' that could be of immense interest to the investors. The IR person must be good in formulating key messages which could be communicated to the investors by various communication channels like, annual reports, web cast, presentations, and even press releases. Besides good story building capabilities, the IR person must be good in positioning the company.

5. Perception Audit: How the investors and analysts perceive the company is of immense use to top officials of the company so that they would know where they stand among the peer group. Accordingly they can identify the areas of improvement and work on measures to re-position themselves and finally benchmark themselves yet again in the peer group.

Table : What is the most difficult aspect of the IRO position?

Market Cap Category	Disclosure	Market Environment	Company Management
Mega	19%	58%	9%
Large	32%	36%	5%
Mid	23%	43%	12%
Small	19%	51%	4%
Micro	19%	49%	3%

Perception Studies Help Understand Investors Concerns

"Perception Studies gather investors' feedback and help to understand their concerns, back to basics in right margin"

- Ashwin Bajaj, Head IR Sterlite Industries

We had an investor perception study performed by an independent firm when management was concerned that we were not getting the value in our stock based on the company's performance at that time to determine the issues we were facing. The results of the first investor perception study indicated that we needed to be more transparent and we needed to communicate our outlook and our guidance / expectations for a longer-term time horizon, and to ensure investors' outlook match our expectations.

An independent firm gathers investor feedback to ensure investors understand our message, whether they accept our message, and what their concerns are. This investor feedback is helpful to management so that they understand the challenges perceived by investors as our management prepares for our quarterly earnings conference calls, one-on-one meetings with investors, and investor conferences. As a result of the investor research intelligence, our investor meetings are more productive and we don't get surprises in meetings with investors on issues we are not prepared for.

Incorporation of results from investor perception studies and feedback reports helps to position the company's message. It is important to have investor perceptions gathered by an independent firm. You can't assume you know what investors are thinking or what concerns are holding investors back from initiating a position or increasing their position in your stock.

The investor can stay anonymous if they would like, which encourages them to be candid. While the feedback may not always be flattering, it is critical for management to learn how investors perceive the company. These reports can help the company think through their strategy and also address any apprehensions or misconceptions.

It is important for a company to understand how investors perceive their company, in order to understand why investors are not investing in the company's stock. Stakeholders may not be totally comfortable giving all their feedback directly during meetings with companies. Hence, a perception study provides them with an opportunity to show their current understanding on the following factors:

1. Business Strategy
2. Future prospects and plans
3. Planned expenditure
4. Contingent liabilities
5. Product and service information
6. Objectives Vs. results
7. Short and long term debt
8. Segment analysis by geography
9. Segment analysis by business activity
10. Statement of cash flows

Back to Basics...

The Investor Education and Protection Fund (IEPF) is funded by government grants and funds from unpaid dividend, mature deposits and debentures, application money.

Institutional Investors Matter

Institutional investors who have the financial muscle are most sought after by the listed companies because their reach extends way beyond their total assets under management as against that of any single individual or a group of private investors' investment decisions. A majority of the assets they manage are long term in nature, hence their investment horizons are long term in nature too.

Since institutions form a fundamental view on a company's long term prospects, they are able to look beyond short term performance. This support offers management sufficient time to execute their strategic plans.

Many institutions have a fiduciary duty to achieve best value for their underlying investors and will only tolerate short term under performance so long as it remains consistent with eventual delivery of long term value.

Table : How frequently does IR Head Travel?

Industry	Quarterly	Weekly
Pharmaceuticals	19%	7%
Financial Services	14%	8%
Hotels	49%	1%
Healthcare	22%	6%
Media & Entertainment	37%	1%
Automobiles	42%	2%
Technology	65%	7%
Telecommunications	68%	3%

"I am completely lost, what kind of guidance can I provide to my investors?"

Institutional Investors do matter

"Senior Management must focus their energies on institutional investors"

-Ramakrishnan, CFO, Sobha Developers

The institutional investors understand the dynamics of the economy, industry, and the company's growth drivers; hence the senior management must focus their time and energies on institutional investors.

The broking companies also organize non-deal road shows wherein either CEO/CFO/IR persons of various companies are invited to attend series of meetings with fund managers from different fund houses.

The Retail investors, on the other hand, are generally small investors and often hold for long term. The returns they look from the company are mostly in the form of dividends, bonus shares, or further investments through rights issues.

In such cases, their needs can be better catered to by the Company Secretary better than the IR Professional. Many of their issues also relate to their individual shareholding issues and not so much about company's performance.

Thus, considering the needs and queries of retail investors will primarily remain the domain of Company Secretaries.

IR is a new generation concept, which is primarily catering to the bulk or institutional investors. To that extent, the Board always supports the IR professional. However, he should not be encouraged to attend the Board meetings, as it is likely that he may get influenced by the discussions conducted at the Board and may inadvertently pose in an unwarranted manner. Further, the company has a Shareholders' and Investors' Grievance Committee which looks into all the shareholders related matters. Therefore, a separate IR committee is not needed.

Table : Does IR work with Communications?

Industry	No
Pharmaceuticals	7%
Financial Services	11%
Textiles	13%
Automobiles	8%
Media & Entertainment	14%
Infrastructure	16%
Technology	6%
Telecommunications	4%

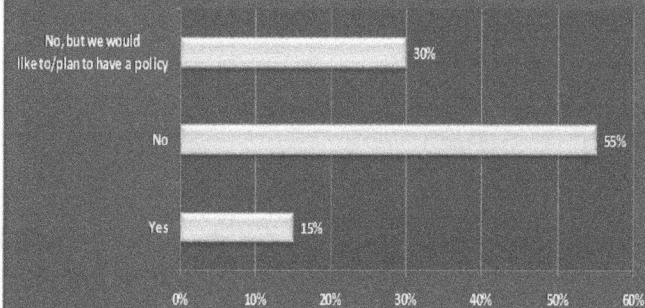

Does your company publish a corporate social responsibility report?

No, but we would like to/plan to have a policy — 30%
No — 55%
Yes — 15%

Managing pooled assets

The asset management of institutional investors operates globally and hence is diverse in terms of the variance in size and depth of funds. These institutions who operate the pooled assets, include venture capital trusts, mutual funds, unit trusts, life assurance and pension plans.

Some funds may offer very specific investment, they could be skewed to a particular country, or industry sector, whereas other funds may only invest in asset classes seeking a specific income level, or specific growth rate. Some funds also base their investment selections on an ethical or corporate social responsibility basis.

Hedge funds: Hedge funds are specialist category of institutional investors whose clients include wealthy individuals. These funds are often lightly regulated, hence they are prohibited to mark their funds to non-professional individual investors.

Benchmarked performance: The fund managers generally benchmark against which they can assess the performance of their funds. These benchmarks are usually a stock market index, the assessment is therefore a relative measure of performance. Out-performance relative to the benchmark is often called alpha by market practitioners. Strategies aimed purely at tracking index, or 'beta', performance are increasingly popular since they are cheaper to pay more in fees to cover the costs.

Back to Basics...

Equity capital may be raised from the promoters, institutional investors such as financial institutions and banks or from the retail public investors.

Benchmarking against peers

"We benchmark ourselves with our international peers"

- Sanjay Shah, CFO, Tree House

We benchmark Tree House only against our international peers as on the domestic companies we do not have any company with our kind of revenue model.

If we have to emerge as a leading global player in pre-school and day care on a self-operating basis then we need to have global standards. Hence, we look at global companies of the likes of Knowledge Universe, Bright Horizon, and Learning Curve as our international peers.

The company currently enjoys a scalable business model, managed to penetrate diverse markets including Tier 2 and 3 cities, and enjoys asset light model resulting in optimization of costs.

The company was able to showcase a de-risked and return focused business model spread over multiple geographies in India with a 5-year CAGR of 73% in revenues and 144% in profits as of FY14.

Back to Basics…

A company raises capital at various stages depending upon the need for equity capital.

Focus on key investors

Is it important for the companies to identify who the shareholders are? IR is all about building relations with shareholders and also targeting prospective investors from the peer group too. Investors come in all shapes and sizes with a multiplicity of requirements, risk tolerances, investment styles and processes. No two investors are the same and may actually approach the purchase of a company's shares from equal and opposite directions.

It is important to assess the risk tolerance of an investor, whether he is seeking regular income or capital gains or both. Some investors do not invest in 'blue sky' companies that are more concept driven; others may follow stock market indices to reduce risk.

Growth vs. Value

The nature of investment process also needs to be analyzed into different categories such as "growth" and "value" although there is a fair degree of overlap between the two. Growth investors will be concerned about growth prospects of the business and hence, anticipate share price performance. The value investor however, looks for companies that are not fancied for now.

Long only institutional investors

The long only institutional investors hold their investments for extended periods, thereby adding respectability to the shareholder register which help to attract other set of investors. On the information gathering front, there are many sources of information like broker written research, personal contact, company announcements, and the internet. But the key determinant is the face to face meeting between the analyst, fund manager and chief executive of the company.

Why are Retail Investors important?

Companies need to seek a diverse range of investors on their share register comprising a range of institutional investors who will invest according to a range of criteria. While the institutions tend to be longer-term investors, the retail investors will comprise those with shorter aspirations. These investors may be driven by changing sentiment towards industry sectors; perceived value opportunities by valuation, by income, or by tax-efficiency. The retail investors often buy in smaller lots thereby providing the required impetus to company's shares by way of liquidity.

Private Investors

The fund managers will be looking at the broad parameters such as the dynamics of the business in which the company operates and its potential growth rates into the future. A comprehensive study of the company's revenue statement, cash-flows, balance sheet, and benchmarking the same against its peers is a prerequisite indeed. This apart, the size of the market in which the company operates, the market share its products enjoy and the likely growth are some of the key factors that the investors look into. Even though it's not advisable, some companies also have private shareholders that buy shares for emotive reasons. These include past and present employees of the company and their families who may possible to measure the 'quality of management'. It can be inferred hence that the fund managers prefer to meet the management before investing so that they can make their own assessment. The organization culture is very important because the same attitude will tomorrow get reflected with its own Investors too.

What Fund Managers will be looking for in companies?

Unlike retail investors, the institutional investors will buy in much bigger lots. Hence, there must be availability of sufficient floating stock. Without liquidity in the markets, it would not be possible to attract institutional investors. The presence of institutional investors on the share register can make a vast difference not only to the company's market cap, but also usher in best practices in investor relations thereby leading to fair valuation.

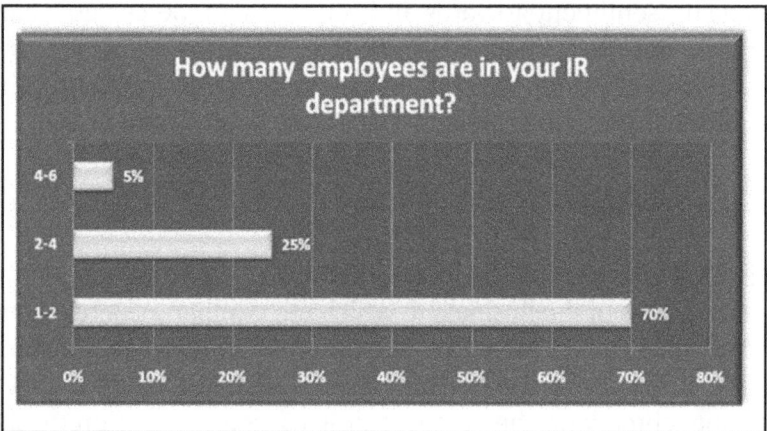

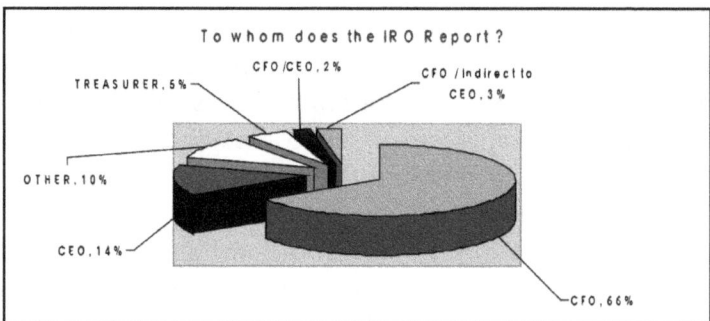

How many employees are in your IR department?

Category	Percentage
4-6	5%
2-4	25%
1-2	70%

To whom does the IRO Report?

- CFO /CEO, 2%
- CFO / Indirect to CEO, 3%
- TREASURER, 5%
- OTHER, 10%
- CEO, 14%
- CFO, 66%

Back to Basics...

Equity capital issues are governed by the regulations of SEBI and the Companies Act and the Listing Agreement.

It's challenging to find Beneficial Owners among FIIs

"In these challenging times where the FIIs operate behind the custodians, it is difficult find out who the real investors are"

- Sandeep Mahindroo, Principal, Infosys

In these challenging times where the Foreign Institutional Investors (FIIs) operate behind their custodians, it's quite a challenge to unveil and find out who your shareholders are!

On Shareholders Identification:

The success story of IR revolves around Precision Targeting of Foreign Institutional Investors (FIIs). These FIIs transact through Custodians, hence the biggest challenge lies in unveiling them and tracing them down to the ultimate decision maker in order to build long term relations with them.

This is where some IR Firms make a significant difference to assist companies to identify the ultimate decision maker among the FIIs through their product called Shareholders Identification. If any Company is not able to sell its story to the FIIs, it will continue to remain a mute spectator to the whims and fancies of few market operators.

FIIs are the prime market movers, as you can see in the figure mentioned here. Hence, zeroing in on their ultimate decision maker is of primary importance without which Investor Relations has no value.

The overall shareholder identification will provide the following information:

- Name of holder (institution);
- Location (city, country);
- Number of shares currently held;
- Corresponding percentage of issued share capital;
- Investment Style ("Growth", "Quantitative", "Hedge Fund", or similar);
- Portfolio Turnover ("High", "Low", "Medium"); and
- Institutional Investment Contact (name, title, telephone number)

Knowledge of shareholders is essential, though not always from a relationship standpoint. It is a basic necessity. Just like a corporation knows its employees and clients, it needs to know its investors also. If the identity of the investors is not known, the company will not be able to reach out to investors and provide access/be accessible to the investor.

A company, though its IR team, needs to be familiar with investors just the investors are expected to be familiar with the company. Unless an IR practitioner knows the profiles of investors, he can't determine the right fit and IR efforts might go waste. Familiarity with the funds' investment profile is highly important; additionally familiarity with the aspects which are key to a fund's investment thesis also helps.

Back to Basics...

The extent of regulation would depend upon the category of investors. The regulations for raising capital from the retail investors are very stringent.

What's the Best Shareholding Base?

One of the primary driving forces for the movement in share values is the buying coming from institutional investors' quarters. These investors buy in large chunks thereby tilting the demand and supply equations. When they buy certain stock, it is seen as good news by the market and this in turn triggers positive momentum. But when these institutions sell, they drive down the share prices. An IR professional in such a scenario has to ensure that there is no en masse selling which may lead to panic among the investors thereby destroying the shareholders wealth.

Some investors hold shares for less time as they prefer to invest their monies only in those stocks which are likely to witness capital appreciation in a shorter period of time. Among all the investors the shortest-term shareholders are the day traders. These day traders buy and sell same stocks on the same day and try to garner returns from trading. Some of them, especially institutions, work with sophisticated trading models to reduce risk.

IR professionals may need to widen their base of investors and attract investors with different investing styles in order to arrest a free fall of share price. They need to target those institutional investors who look for long term growth stories. Investors such as these do not look around only for immediate momentum in the stock prices, instead they bet on hard-core fundamental analysis, the commitment of top management towards the company and its shareholders, and their track record in steering the company to higher levels.

Amongst the institutional investors some of them have dedicated funds for mid cap and small cap portfolios. History also goes to show that at times small cap companies have the wherewithal to outperform the market. The Investment Discipline of these investors is very important for a company.

It is of course possible for the companies to scrutinize and categorize the institutional investors into long term and short term investors by analyzing their portfolio turnover levels. The momentum investors, for instance, may churn their portfolios over several times a year, while institutions which stand by purely fundamentals models may at best churn only about 30% of their portfolio annually.

In this backdrop, what ought to be a good mix between institutional and individual investors for a company? There is no definite answer, but a good blend of retail investors and institutional investors is always advisable.

There is no ideal Shareholding base. If you can determine an ideal shareholder base, you can take steps toward achieving it. But it's a very complicated issue because 'x' percent concentration of a particular type of investor isn't right for everyone. An investor has to marry a company's fundamentals with the complementary shareholder base.

While the IR Heads and CFOs want to have longer-term investors, it turns out that the best-performing companies actually have a marginally higher proportion of short-term investors. Before one can determine the ideal investor mix, there is an urgent need to have a good basic handle on their existing shareholder base.

IROs hire consultants to help them identify shareholders so that they can get some additional useful information pertaining to the price at which the shareholders had bought shares which would give a rough indication on the probable exit price.

The Shareholder Identification, on the other hand, is a very important tool which will help to identify the ultimate decision makers in the FIIs which otherwise invest through the custodians. Knowing investors will help in projecting their likely voting pattern either in favor or against at the Annual General Meetings

The companies must give a careful thought to their investment story over the medium to long term. They also need to detail out on what they are planning to do with their cash flow i.e., will they return to shareholders via buybacks, dividends, or thrive on acquisitions. Accordingly, a very effective road map for shareholding base can be laid down.

Who are private investors?

These are retail investors who buy shares either directly without taking professional advice or they may pay for advice from a private client stockbroker and buy shares on their recommendation. A part of private investors also include company's own employees who became shareholders via employee stock options or by purchasing shares via company-sponsored schemes. They have invested directly, or hold (now converted) share options that are often retained for reasons of loyalty or sentimentality hence, the presence of senior management at road shows becomes important.

Targeting private investors

All quoted companies must have an effective annual investor relations program. This must include a proactive approach to communication with stock market constituents in order to maintain visibility with existing and potential investors.

The role of the media and private investors

In addition to an annual investor relations programme, companies may also hire services of a financial public relations adviser to hone the message to investors and the media and in gaining media coverage in the right places, at the right time. National newspapers give increasingly less space to routine company news and results, whereas there is a wide range of magazines and websites targeted specifically at private investors.

Again, coverage in these can be crucial in terms of stimulating interest in, and demand for, a company's shares from private investors.

The internet too has transformed investor relations practice for companies. Several front-running companies maintain a comprehensive investor section on the business on their website. Through the corporate website, many companies encourage e-mail communication from investors. The corporate website also provides a platform for efficiently providing private investors with information and updates about the company.

Conclusion

The interest and support of private client brokers and private investors are vital in stimulating demand for shares and with it, potential liquidity.

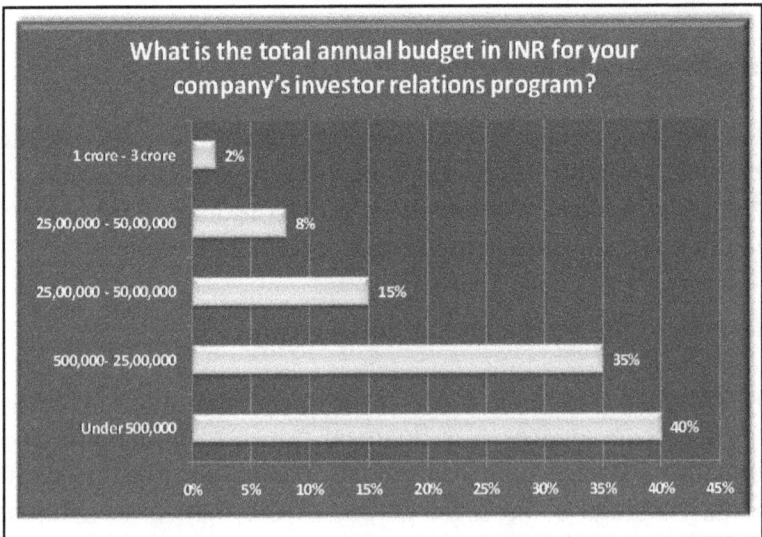

What is the total annual budget in INR for your company's investor relations program?

Category	Percentage
1 crore - 3 crore	2%
25,00,000 - 50,00,000	8%
25,00,000 - 50,00,000	15%
500,000 - 25,00,000	35%
Under 500,000	40%

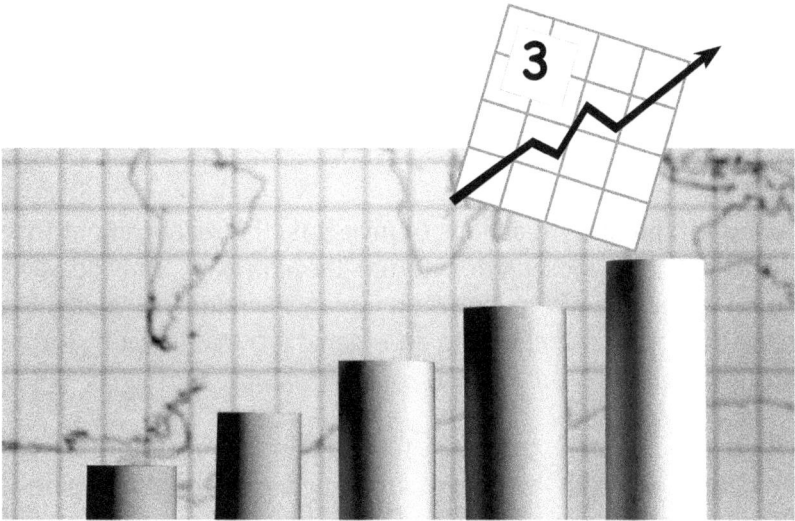

3

Investor Relations Strategy

IR Methodology

In matured capital market economies like the US and UK, IR is being increasingly seen as essential strategic function. Be it the surveys of shareholders, road-shows, reverse road-shows, analyst meetings, conference calls, annual reports, and others, these are being viewed as tools to learn about your shareholders, communicate and build relationships.

IR helps develop the companies to chalk out strategic course of action thereby facilitating critical decision making process. This move ushers in a broader acceptance of the management's action to help grow the company.

IR Process can be maximized with a 2 - dimensional approach: 1. Disseminating investors with the complete story so that the company is well understood and fairly valued; and 2. Giving valuable feedback to the management from the investors, analysts, and others whose opinion matters so that it will help the management to focus on brand-building exercise in the investors' community.

Based on the likely reactions of investors, the management may decide on a viable way to nurture the company. The decision could range anywhere between giving dividends or ploughing back the resources, choosing an organic growth or opting for an inorganic growth and scouting for acquisitions.

Ultimately investor's opinion is reflected in their decisions to buy, hold, and sell. With the help of strong network with shareholders, IR professionals can solicit feedback from the investors on the future course of action and take up appropriate steps.

Key factors of IR Program

A successful IR program shall comprise comprehensive strategy to realize benefits to the full length. IR primarily consists of about 4 crucial points that need to be developed. These key factors include:

1. Capital Market Research: to gain in depth knowledge and expertise in capital markets, investment process, investor behavior, investor perceptions and attitudes toward the company, and to track progress in the communications process.

2. Information Hub: disseminating vital information and interpreting the same to investors and institutions which matter will help in getting fair valuations.

3. Right kind of Communication Channels: using right kind

of Communication Channels is important for making the information reach to a logical conclusion wherein the investors, analysts, and brokers, are kept updated.

4. Office Administration: employing the right kind of technology, staff, and consultants, will help manage the IR process more efficiently.

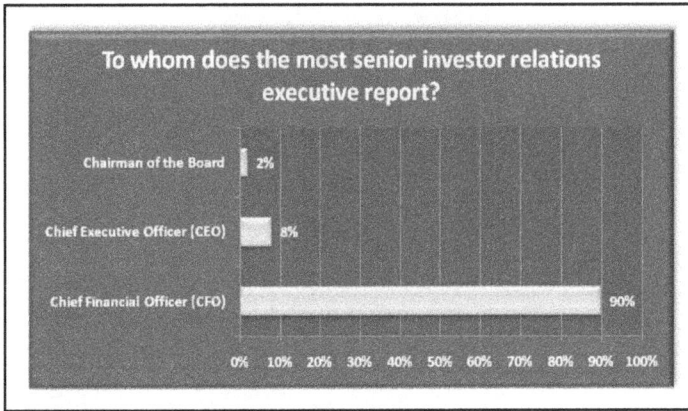

To whom does the most senior investor relations executive report?

Chairman of the Board	2%
Chief Executive Officer (CEO)	8%
Chief Financial Officer (CFO)	90%

Table : How long do analyst meetings last?

Industry	1-3 Hrs
Pharmaceuticals	12%
Business Services	0%
Financial Services	41%
Energy	4%
Hotel	0%
Healthcare	17%
Media & Entertainment	0%
Automobiles	13%
Technology	6%
Telecommunications	0%

I R Program will be successful if there is a clear strategy

"We have a 4 pronged IR strategy"

- Dinesh Thapar, Head Investor Relations,
Hindustan Uniliver

Our Investor Relations program is guided by a clear IR strategy and is fundamentally anchored around four key thrusts namely, sharpening the investment case/messaging, focusing the engagement, high quality IR tools/practices and bringing the outside in. While we have made progress on all four dimensions, the one specific area that I'd like to talk about here is how we are applying technology to raise the bar across the breadth of our Investor Relations function in recent times –

We are increasingly leveraging technology (virtual formats like video conferencing and telepresence) for investor engagements – this has twin fold benefits of efficiency and flexibility and works well in a context where we have stepped up our level of engagement with investors across the world.

With investors and analysts constantly on the move, to facilitate ease and regularity of access, we have developed investor apps (HUL Investor) for smart phones and tablets on both iOS and Android platforms. The apps can be downloaded directly from the iStore/Playstore.

Companies must interact with as many shareholders and non-shareholders as possible, which, in the case of reaching private investors, usually involves structured visits to key regional cities where there are concentrations of private broking firms. A company must selectively interact with its investors on a quarterly basis and invite all its shareholders for the company's Annual General Meeting and encourage active participation in the question answer session.

We have also invested behind significantly upgrading our Investor Relations website and building Online Annual Reports which incorporate the best in class functionality. Both of these were recognized by the Investor Relations Global Rankings (IRGR) in the 2012 edition.

Whilst being adjudged to have the Best Online Annual Report in India in the 2012 IRGR edition, this is clearly one of the areas where we have continued to raise the bar by dramatically upgrading functionality and incorporating features from some of the best online annual reports across the world. The Interactive HUL Online Annual Report for FY 2012-13 can be accessed at http://hulannualreports.co.in/arinhtml/in-500696/2013/ar_eng_2013/index.html.

Recognizing that a number of our investors are based in the Western world and that they may not be able to connect into our investor events due to time zone differences, we have since the last year, moved to a solution which provides a replay immediately after the event in addition to the transcript. The technology is being deployed for our quarterly earnings calls and was also used earlier this year for the HUL Annual Investor Meet. While these are some examples to make the point, it is our intent to keep applying technology to drive our Investor Relations program with continued impact whilst remaining efficient.

Back to Basics...

SEBI's guidelines lay down the norms for eligibility norms for companies to raise capital from the public.

Information Hub

Insights into capital markets will help in understanding the information needs to properly value the company. Timely quality information needs to be given. The information obviously should focus on all those aspects that make your company a good investment.

Since investors are essentially looking for higher returns, current share price of the company is not an area of concern for them but the future value of the scrip definitely is. They invest in shares anticipating a raise in revenues and earnings. When companies improve margins to create higher earnings, the excess cash is either re-invested into the company to capture growth opportunities or used to buy back shares or to step up dividends. Investors analyze companies to determine how companies will achieve these financial gains. This in turn becomes the company's value driver.

Some of the value drivers could be as follows:

- Production efficiencies that can make the company a low-cost producer.
- Margins that would usher in price advantage and higher profitability.
- Ability to deliver superior customer service compared to its peers.
- Technology that enables the company to innovate, creates new products, and maintains a lead in terms of quality.
- Smart management that creates result-oriented environment.
- Financial strategists good at deal making which enables them to access cheaper funds and save money.
- Series of acquisitions leading to stronger product base, expanded markets, new applications for technology and grabbing more market share.

- Highly skilled and motivated marketing and sales team.

The disclosure dilemma

It's a Catch 22 situation for the company's management when it comes to disclosures. While wrong disclosure may trigger a law suit, inadequate disclosure too may attract a lawsuit. Optimistically speaking, adequate disclosure alone helps in unlocking full valuation.

A right kind of disclosure policy shall help in improving investors' perception, getting the right kind of shareholder mix, reducing cost of capital, and maximizing shareholder value.

Consistent information disclosure attracts sell-side analyst coverage and they start relying on the information coming from company's sources, ultimately leading to a better consensus in the analyst community.

Extensive analyst coverage also helps lure hoards of informed investors with fair amount of expectations and they would also have consensus in expectations, thereby helping the firm reduce its cost of capital. Thus, the benefits of disclosure offset the risks and even the costs (if the company were to get sued for not adequately disclosing or for wrong disclosure).

Through adequate and timely disclosures, companies enhance their market value by disclosing information relating to: business collaborations; new product pipeline; capital investments; advances on the technological front; and others.

Information could be structured or unstructured. Mandated documents like prospectus, audited financials, directors report and management discussion and analysis in annual reports, are some of the documents that are structured and must be provided in a precise manner.

Unstructured disclosure relates to all that information which is made available to the outside world through communication channels like investors' meets, teleconference, speeches, web sites, letters to shareholders, and others.

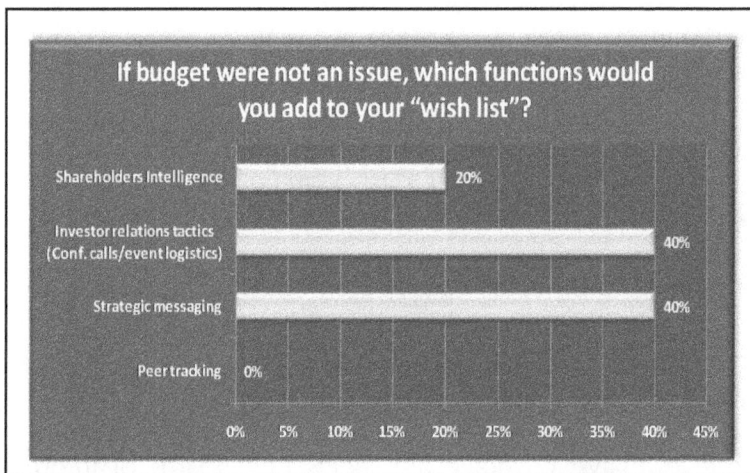

If budget were not an issue, which functions would you add to your "wish list"?

Function	Value
Shareholders Intelligence	20%
Investor relations tactics (Conf. calls/event logistics)	40%
Strategic messaging	40%
Peer tracking	0%

"Loyalty like you? Will Investors appreciate?"

CSR report provides information about social, environmental and economic performance

"Allocation of 2% profits to CSR activities is welcome"

- AK Banerjee, Director Finance, ONGC

The concept of 'Sustainability' holds importance in this domain whereby companies show the contributions to the society and environment. Whilst the financial objective of the companies is maximizing stakeholder's wealth, the corporate social responsibility should contain measures taken by companies impacting stakeholders like consumer, employees, government, shareholders, society, suppliers, vendors etc. The key topics that should be covered in the CSR report include:

a) Key risk areas and opportunities.
b) Management systems for sustainability
c) Organization profile and product portfolio.
d) Governance, commitments and engagements with stakeholders
e) Value addition for business partners.
f) Labor practices etc.

The proposed provision of allocation of 2 % of profits for CSR activities is a welcome measure proposed by Company Law Bill which aims at promoting social responsibility amongst the

companies. There is a moral obligation of the companies to provide adequate returns to the society for using the relevant resources. This would ensure part of profits being appropriated for social causes.

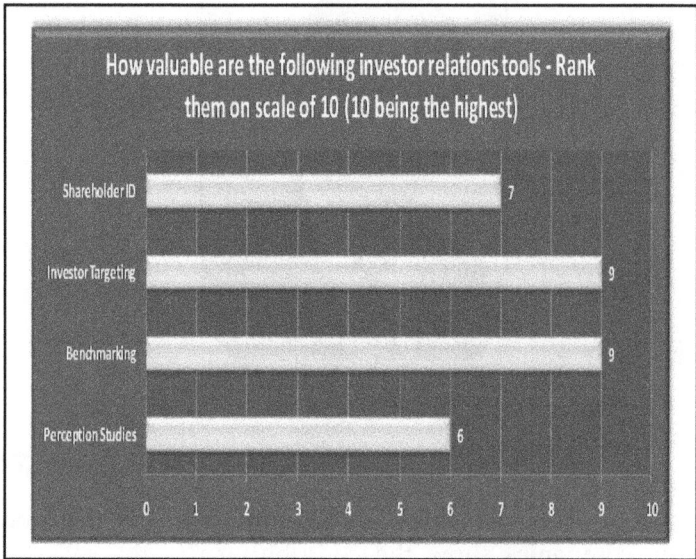

How valuable are the following investor relations tools - Rank them on scale of 10 (10 being the highest)

Tool	Rank
Shareholder ID	7
Investor Targeting	9
Benchmarking	9
Perception Studies	6

"We practice 'out of the box' thinking to raise money from investors"

Role of Analyst

Sell-side Analysts: work for investment banks and stockbrokers. Their research is distributed to institutional and other investors. Sell-side analysts will aim to achieve high ranking in external institutional voting surveys in order to maximize the impact of their research. Sell-side analysts look to generate share-trading commission revenue from institutional investors.

Buy-side Analysts: are employed by fund management institutions to provide specialist knowledge for internal usage by the fund managers in guiding their investment decisions. Their forecasts are not publicly available.

As companies listed on bourses do not generally publish their own earnings guidance, the sell-side analysts play a vital role in setting market expectations on likely profitability and future growth. This can also be used as a benchmarking for judging the performance among the peer group in a specific sector of companies.

The company too must remain conscious of the market's expectations of its performance and immediately inform the market if they become aware that they are likely to diverge materially from consensus analyst forecasts, this makes the Perception Studies essential.

The regulations create a situation where listed companies do not explicitly set their own forecasts or expectations but are judged by their ability to meet the market's expectation of their performance, as observed by the analysts. An analyst will publish opinions on a company, following a company's publication of results, trading updates or corporate activity.

Best IR Practices Lead to Higher PE Multiples

"Companies that follow Best Practices in IR, enjoy higher PE Multiples"

- Arnob Mondal, Vice President, Investor Relations, L&T

Companies that follow best practices in IR typically tend to enjoy higher market multiples compared to their peers. The multiples could be PE, P/B, EV/EBITDA or any appropriate valuation multiple. The important practices that facilitate this are –

Transparency and disclosure – apart from building confidence in company management, this ensures that there are minimal black boxes that markets have to grapple with in understanding operations of the Company.

Strong outreach program – this ensures wide coverage of markets and hence enhances a potential investment case to a multitude of capital market participants across different geographies.

Knowledge of the Company (business models, strategy, processes) – this gives a strong foundation to capital markets on understanding the Company and enables markets to make superior valuation calls on the Company

Knowledge of the industry – this adds contextual flavour to company business models and ensures that the management story is not articulated in a vacuum without any external interface. Markets also value this since it serves an educative purpose and, in a way, is a transparent enumeration of how the Company functions in a given environment.

Financial knowledge – this clearly gives sharp focus and granularity to brokers and investors that enables them to fine-tune and refine valuations.

Superior communication skills – this enhances acuity of understanding in the minds of market participants.

Enabling interface with business heads in a controlled environment – this gives much better depth to brokers and investors since business heads have richer domain knowledge about their own businesses

Guidance and forewarning – markets appreciate our telling them in advance about expected key parameters since valuations are ultimately exercises in trying to pin down future numbers.

The above are some of the things that we believe add value to capital markets. Markets, in turn, reward corporates (who follow these practices) with superior multiples and less scrip volatility. Just as equity markets should ideally be broad and deep, company understanding should also be broad and deep if valuations of the company are to be fair, proper and reasonable – IR best practices enable this. Since levels of IR standards in these areas vary from company to company, market multiples also tend to vary (and to some extent in line with IR standards). While this is not an exact science, a correlation does exist.

Back to Basics...

A private placement of shares in the form of a preferential allotment or a Qualified institutional placement imposes less regulatory compliances on the company.

Domains of Information

Various domains of information sought after by the investors and analysts originate from the company's strategies, strengths and programs. Information falls into three categories: (1) financial and operational details (2) company's vision and its broad strategies and (3) industry context of the company.

Some specific minute details regarding to the company's operations is of immense use to the analysts for projecting the company's performance in the near-term. Details could include information like: inventory shipments, new and lost contracts, SG&A, receivables, payables, and so on and so forth.

Analysts and investors look out for financial performance categorized on the basis of businesses, products, geographical regions, and other such parameters. This kind of information will help in understanding as to which of the business division is the largest, highest contributor to the company's bottom-line etc. This data shall help in evaluating whether the management is investing in the growth areas or whether it is pumping in resources in areas of lesser growth.

The research firm, Shelley Taylor & Associates, every year makes it a point to ask about 100 professional investors to identify important information obtainable from companies. The top 10 in the list includes:

1. Business Strategy
2. Future prospects and plans
3. Planned expenditure
4. Contingent liabilities
5. Product and service information
6. Objectives vs. results
7. Short and long-term debt
8. Segment analysis by geography

9. Segment analysis by business activity
10. Statement of cash flows

Typical areas covered in analyst reports:

Analysts need to have deep an understanding of a company, its key drivers and macro influences. Towards this end, they regularly seek access to the company's management and ongoing direct communication. This is important for their understanding of historic financial, particularly if there were one off events that effected performance in the past. Company's plant visits, depending on the type of company, are often useful for increasing their knowledge base. Some analysts also like to have access to the larger customers of the company to increase their understanding of future growth prospects.

Many analysts look for an information edge over their competitors, which allows them to generate interest. Since analysts differ in their opinion on a company's future performance, there is a need to take an average of all the analysts' forecasts on a particular stock to have a 'consensus'. The analysts' forecast is compared against the consensus number, in order to figure out the deviation if any from the consensus number.

Consensus Estimates: Different analysts focus on different aspects of a company's performance. Some analysts, for instance, will place emphasis on the gross profit than EBITDA or PAT. This apart, certain numbers will be more relevant depending on the sector such as the sales density figure for the retail sector etc.

Treatment of goodwill, royalty payments and pension interest also differs among analysts, leading to use of judgment in arriving at consensus estimates. This complicates the calculation of consensus figures, as do out-of-date forecasts which can distort the situation. The sell side research reports notes are targeted mainly at the institutional fund manager. Often, they will use a wide variety of brokers' reports to get the full spectrum of market opinion on a company and also challenge their own views. Fund managers generally trust only a handful of analysts whom they rate high on their models and forecasts.

Analyst coverage

A majority of analysts have a sector focus and therefore need to cover a good number of companies within that sector in order to speak with authority and understand the sector dynamics. The decision will also depend on a company's market capitalization, daily average trading volumes and the stock's overall liquidity. For example, if a company has a small number of shares readily available, it may not make any sense for a broking company to bring out a research report as these are meant only for institutional investors who will buy chunk of shares from the market.

Companies with a market capitalization below Rs 1000 crore enjoy research coverage from say 1 to 4 analysts. Those companies with a market capitalization between Rs 1000 crore to 10,000 crore may be tracked by at least 20 analysts. These companies either have dedicated IR divisions or external IR consultancy divisions or both.

On an average, retail investors are dramatically different from institutional investors. The institutional investors take market drops, bad earnings, economic shocks and so on as part of normal business unlike the retail investors.

As a fund manager, you see problems all the time, and one of the key tenets of the job is dealing with various issues that pop up at your investee companies. Even if a company misses earnings estimates, the fund managers know how to deal with it.

The retail investors however, worry about everything because their own personal future is at stake. Individuals worry about every block trade, every insider selling report, every analyst's suggestion; however, not everything is important. Just because there is a press release does not mean the news is worth reading. Sometimes, executives need to sell shares, and it does not mean the company is about to collapse.

Table : How often do you meet overseas investors?

Industry	Annually	Never
Pharmaceuticals	40%	15%
Financial Services	8%	69%
Hotel	18%	67%
Healthcare	21%	58%
Media & Entertainment	16%	51%
Automobiles	18%	65%
Technology	57%	43%
Telecommunications	21%	79%

"I wish my company's share price too sailed so smoothly on markets"

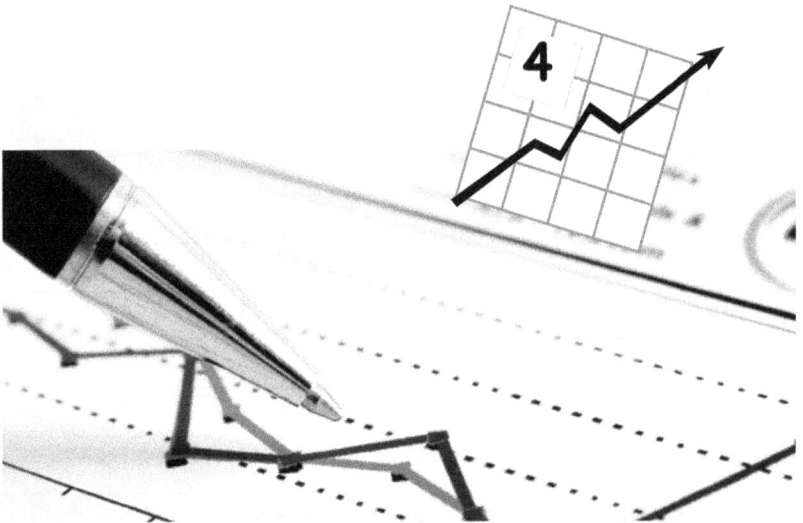

4

The Influence of Financial Journalists

Financial media coverage will foster visibility for a company and acts as a backdrop to its IR program. It plays an influential role as it's relied upon by investors and the public to assess the 'invest ability' of companies. The need for companies to communicate effectively to this audience and ultimately to all shareholders is paramount.

IR professionals are in the business of establishing and protecting reputations; financial commentators are in the business of questioning these and attempting to put a true value on these reputations. Good financial PR will act as a conduit between a company and the financial media, and help this process.

It is a far cheaper way of building a company's reputation than advertising, with the added benefit of being a third party (journalist's) opinion, which adds credibility.

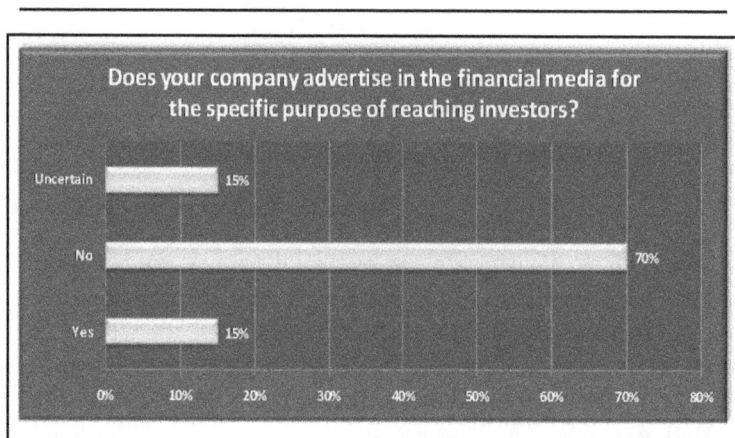

Does your company advertise in the financial media for the specific purpose of reaching investors?

Uncertain	15%
No	70%
Yes	15%

"Its payback time friends, we thrived at the expense of investors so far..."

Communication skills is the need of the hour

"CFOs need to improve communication skills"

- Ganapathy Subramanian, CFO,Hathaway

The CFOs, IR professionals are essential to any corporation that needs to keep its finances on track and ensure it makes the best business decisions possible. But a major chunk of CFOs and IR Professionals have a Chartered Accountancy background, hence, even though they are good at number crunching, they are not very articulative.

Many people think that there is a need for just the concrete skills in accounting and finance, but they need some soft skills like that of communication in order to be successful in their positions.

Almost 70% of the meetings with the investors pertain to non-deal road shows, hence CFOs/IRPs must be extremely articulative. If they are unable to articulate, then the CFOs must seek assistance from Investor Relations professionals.

Besides external communications, the CFOs/IRP must also be communicative internally too. For instance, it is helpful to have a CFO/IRP who's been in a variety of positions, taken on numerous different responsibilities, worked on multiple teams and understands what other company employees go through on a daily basis.

Some companies have put their CFOs/IRPs in charge of IT budgets too. This means a financial officer needs to be willing to take on projects that may not be directly related to their area of expertise in order to ensure a corporation's operations run smoothly. Being able to understand IT analytics projects, automated data reporting, cloud technology and big data can not only help them to manage projects, but also help them steer a business in the right direction.

Table : Is IR part of a rotational program?

Industry	Proactive
Pharmaceuticals	90%
Financial Services	69%
Hotel	89%
Healthcare	64%
Media & Entertainment	91%
Automobiles	88%
Technology	82%
Telecommunications	78%

Does your company send out prepared remarks in advance of the earnings conference call?

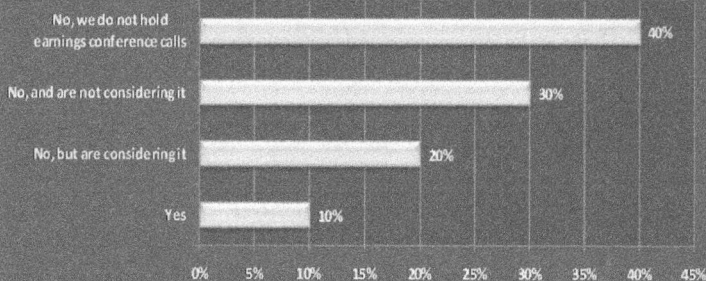

Response	Percentage
No, we do not hold earnings conference calls	40%
No, and are not considering it	30%
No, but are considering it	20%
Yes	10%

The journalist's agenda

For a company to communicate effectively to the media, it is imperative that its IR representatives understand the dynamics of the financial journalist's agenda, so that the engagement runs smoothly and effectively for both, the company and the journalist. The recent rise in demand for financial and business news has resulted in a significant increase in workload for financial journalists due to the internet era too. Meeting deadlines is a crucial part of the journalist's trade, which means a fast response from IR advisers is essential.

DIFFERENT NEWS will require different approaches to the media. Before any meeting, the IR adviser's briefing to the management is essential. Key announcements need to be released to the market. Annual and interim results are major opportunities to engage with the media. Other events that might spark communication include announcements of key contracts or new business and Board appointments.

Mere financial numbers is dry material; hence, some more supporting material will add color to a story and increase its attraction to a journalist. Using materials such as quotations, photography and statistics to illustrate a trend or issue more effectively can all form an effective part of a financial strategy to engage a journalist.

Negative news will sometimes emerge and companies should work with their IR advisers to mitigate any potential damage. Every company should have a media policy in place, and ensure that only one person talks to the media.

Even when journalists are writing negative stories, it pays to be polite, helpful and truthful. Companies need to display openness and maintain a constructive dialogue with all key stakeholders, including the media, particularly in difficult times. This strategy will benefit the business the most.

Rating of Analysts

Thomson Reuters and Bloomberg terminals rate sell-side analysts based on the quality of research reports they put out. There are also various kinds of awards to support these ratings. Investor Relations Society, India too did IR Awards recently with Thomson Reuters at BSE and with IRGR in London Stock Exchange.

The question is should the IR Professionals from various companies too be part of the jury that gives awards to sell-side analysts? IR Professionals like Pritish Vinay and several others feel that even their feedback must be considered and currently these awards are only based on opinions of funds.

"I want to look taller like my share price..."

Back to Basics...

Other constituents such as the R&T agent, bankers and underwriters are appointed by the lead manager in consultation with the company. All constituents have to be the entities registered with SEBI.

IR Professionals too must have a say in recognizing sell-side analysts

*"IR Professionals must play an active role in deciding
the awards for sell-side analysts"*

- Pritish Vinay, IR Head, JSW

At a time when the buyside (fund managers) plays a prominent role in voting at various Investor Relations Award events, Pritish Vinay, IR Head, JSW, feels that even IR professionals must have a say at Analyst Awards events.

Excerpts:

Do you think IR Heads must be involved in rating analysts?

Yes absolutely. While undertaking the broker-run non-deal road shows, we, in any case have our parameters to judge which include: brokers with current research coverage on your company and the ability to provide own targets. There is hence nothing wrong if analysts are also rated by IR Heads.

What are the major goals of your IR Program?

Our goals include: increase institutional holdings; increase FIIs holdings; increase research coverage; improve liquidity; increase retail ownership; provide intelligence to the Board.

How is the performance of IR team measured?

An IR Professional's performance is measured through: quality of information in analyst reports; perception studies; shareholder composition; number of new shareholders; and management of share price.

What type of market intelligence does IR department provide to management?

The market intelligence comprises: sellside analyst opinions; peer information; market trends; industry trends; stock performance; and media mentions.

What types of guidance does your company provide?

We provide guidance on: capex; revenues; earnings; margins; non-financial goals; and cash flows.

Which criteria do you use to select a broker for a non-deal road show?

Following criteria is used to select a broker for a non-deal road show: geographical presence; quality of research; ability to identify new investors; and investment banking relationships.

Which criteria are used to target new equity investors?

Some of the strategies used include: investment style; peer ownership; industry focus; equity assets under management.

Back to Basics...

The lead manager gets in-principle approval of the stock exchange, files the draft prospectus with SEBI, files the final prospectus with the RoC and ensures compliance with SEBI's regulations.

The Investor Relations Team

The investment community places significant emphasis on the quality of a company's Board, and in particular,. its management team. Institutional investors may well insist on meeting key management prior to investing, and will expect to maintain a dialogue with the company's Chief Executive and Finance Director. Effectively, this means that these directors will have to commit time to meeting and speaking with shareholders, potential investors, sell-side analysts and journalists. Although companies will involve their advisers, the investor relations function cannot be outsourced wholesale.

Despite investor contact naturally being more concentrated

around the publication of company results, it is not uncommon for Chief Executives and Finance Directors to spend 10pc – 20pc of their annual time on investor relations. Needless to say, the time allocated for IR activities will depend on a number of factors – the number of shareholders in the company, whether the share register mostly comprises institutional or private investors and whether the company is actively seeking new investors, as well as the level of news flow and company announcements. The direct contact with investors, company management and investor relations personnel will also need to allocate time with sell-side analysts and the media.

The time to be committed will also depend on the level to which the company wishes to raise its profile. The IR activities may also extend for a company as it grows in size, profile and following. Larger sized companies, as well as those with either a very large or internationally dispersed following, will normally employ an IR professional to support the Board with activities like preparing investor presentations, company announcements, website content and liaising with the company's advisers.

In the mid and small sized companies it is typically the CFO and CEO who carry out these activities with assistance from the Company Secretary to some extent. Be it the large, mid and small sized companies, a company's Board should regularly review the company's IR strategy and evaluate if its current IR programme is meeting its objectives or there is some kind of shortfall in terms of the expectations.

Company Management

The Companies Act states that every company must keep a register of its members. A good registrar will:

- Maintain the company's register of members and handle shareholder transactions and queries
- Provide an interface to share-trade settlement providers

- Make payments, including actioning dividends
- Manage corporate actions, such as capital raisings, mergers and acquisitions
- Distribute information about the company to its shareholders
- Aid industry and market development.

Listed companies monitor share ownership either via the registrar or IR consultancy firms in shareholder analysis on a regular basis. This analysis of the register is important during an AGM, corporate action or in trying to spot stock predators. While devising an IR programme, the register of members is the starting point and it helps to understand who they are and who has chosen not to invest. This also helps to unearth the underlying beneficial holders below the custodian.

Registrars

Registrars are the one touch point between retail investors and companies. Registrars dispatch electronic copies of statutory documents to shareholders and e-mail broadcasts of pre-scheduled company publications. Some registrars also offer on and offline printing and annual report design and production. Registrars usually provide a comprehensive package of meeting solutions essentially designed to support every stage of the process, from proxy card design, printing and distribution to vote collation and reporting of results. This apart, the registrars might also offer technology solutions including electronic hand-held voting.

On the employee share plans and share options management too, registrars play an important role. Such plans can also be a useful tool in attracting and retaining staff. Web-based tools enable shareholders to easily and effectively manage their investment portfolio.

Share-dealing services- Registrars often have the ability to offer comprehensive share-dealing programs, which include dividend reinvestment and register reduction programs.

Proxy Solicitation may not happen for now

"Proxy Solicitation will take a while to catch up in India.
A majority of companies are promoter-controlled unlike their counterparts in developed countries"

- Shriram Subramanium, MD, InGovern

The IR advisers must anticipate the questions that will be asked and be well prepared with answers supported by facts and figures. The journalists at times may call companies in late hours if they believe they have unearthed something crucial. In this situation, IR advisers should be working with a company's management with pre-agreed responses ready. It pays to treat journalists as important and very demanding customers, and that way, a company is more likely to get a favorable result.

A positive relationship with smooth lines of communication generates goodwill between a company and media, and should go a long way to ensuring that a company has its fair share of voice in the media. Companies should try to engage with media in a positive manner.

Excerpts of an interview with Shriram Subramanium, MD, InGovern, the country's first proxy advisory firm

IR Society: Shareholders these days are asking more polished and tricky questions at AGMs, thanks to the advent of Proxy Advisors firms like that of yours. But don't you think that the government must bring in a "level playing field" for the corporates and usher in Proxy Solicitation service?

Shriram: It is the right of shareholders to ask questions, whether proxy advisory firms exist or not. Promoters and managements of companies have yet to consider minority shareholders as long-term partners that they need to provide answers to. After all, it is the company that has raised money from capital markets. If companies are uncomfortable answering questions, they shouldn't list and raise funds from other shareholders.

Whether proxy solicitation services exist or not, it is a level-playing field. The Indian corporate structure is still largely promoter controlled and hence, most of the variety of ways including one-to-one meetings throughout the corporate calendar and not just at results resolutions that are put to vote are easily passed without much resistance from minority shareholders, even though such resolutions may not be in the best interests of minority shareholders. This is unlike developed markets, where the promoter holding is lesser comparatively and hence, the board needs to resort to proxy solicitation to pass major resolutions, especially against activist and possibly dissident shareholders.

In India, all listed companies have not even achieved the minimum public shareholding norms as laid down by SEBI and hardly does any minority retail investor vote in company resolutions. In such a scenario, proxy solicitation will only help the promoters. If allowed legally, then these companies will formally be able to solicit more minority votes using company's funds. We need to first attain a corporate environment with more diversified shareholding structure along with increased institutional and shareholder activism before we can introduce proxy solicitations for Indian companies.

Although, with the advent of proxy advisory firms such as InGovern, shareholder activism and opposition from non-controlling shareholders have increased in recent times, we still have a lot to catch up in terms of board structure, control, governance practices, etc and greater institutional investor involvement in governance matters.

Having said the above, proxy solicitation can also help listed companies to improve investor relations and become more transparent, if disclosures for proxy solicitation are made more stringent. In developed markets, corporate issuers need to send out detailed information statement to their shareholders while soliciting proxies.

IR Society: Proxy Solicitation firms help corporates in analyzing the pulse of shareholders and the likely voting pattern at the AGMs so that they, the corporates will not be in for a rude shock at the AGMs. Don't you think the current Companies Act which prohibits companies from soliciting proxies must be abolished?

Shriram: Proxy solicitation firms help corporate issuers understand their shareholder base and their voting patterns in company meetings, especially from institutional shareholders. In addition to voting intelligence and reports, proxy solicitation firms also ensure higher vote participation in meetings.

However, as stated earlier, the Indian context is a little different form the developed markets. Unlike in developed markets, we do not have an environment of hostile takeovers or shareholder activism, where bad management is replaced by dissenting or powerful shareholders. Cases like Satyam, Kingfisher, Deccan Chronicle, etc are classic examples. Since the majority shareholding is controlled by promoters, most of the resolutions are passed without much opposition. We need to first attain a corporate environment with a more diversified shareholding structure along with an increased institutional and shareholder activism before we can introduce proxy solicitations in Indian companies.

IR Society: Internationally how is the relation between Proxy Advisory firms and Proxy Solicitation firms?

Shriram: In developed markets, proxy advisory firms play a very important role and influence how most of the institutional investors vote. Hence, companies or issuers generally engage proxy solicitation firms for their general meetings to deal with proxy advisory firms as well as institutional investors to understand their voting proposals for meetings. The relation between proxy advisory

firms and proxy solicitation firms is congenial as proxy solicitation firms realize that proxy advisory firms influence voting to a large extent. Also, talent moves between these two sets of firms.

IR Society: The general perception is that a majority of Indian promoters hold a major chunk of shares hence, they may be able to push the resolutions in their favour. What has been the experience of InGovern? Percentage-wise in how many cases were they able to oppose the resolutions?

Shriram: Indian companies have seen a lot of shareholder activism and opposition from non-controlling shareholders in company resolutions in recent times, especially since proxy advisory firms such as InGovern have started coming out with vote recommendations for such investors. A few recent examples are listed below:

* 23.15% of votes were against the merger of 3 promoter controlled unlisted entities with Akzo Nobel India.
* More than 20% valid shareholders of Sesa Goa voted against the merger of Sesa Goa, Sterlite and other unlisted entities of the Vedanta Group
* 60.36% of valid votes of non-institutional shareholders voted against the merger of Satyam Computers and Mahindra Satyam.
* Certain shareholders having aggregate voting rights of more than 5% in Halonix complained to EBI/ED over the company's violations of FEMA and misleading public shareholders
* UK based hedge fund TCI filed a case against Coal India's Board for its rollback of price increase under government's directives

This shows increasingly positive signs of increased shareholder activism in India. However, we have noticed that in spite of such large opposition from minority shareholders and growing engagement by institutional investors on corporate governance matters, these resolutions get passed due to large promoter holdings in these companies.

Corporate Broker

The broker is responsible for advice on the sizing, timing and pricing of any capital raising, including IPO, rights issues, placings and open offers, and block trades. This apart, some broker's also undertake investor education, and marketing to domestic and international institutional investors in the allocation and pricing of offerings. A key element of the brokerage service involves connecting companies with existing and new institutional investors through coordinated road shows where companies meet investors in a series of one-to-one and group meetings in key investor locations.

The corporate broker's IR team also receives inputs from the research and sales teams whose knowledge and insights are gained from close interaction with institutions. Corporate brokers bring Market knowledge- the most important requirement is that the broker provides in-depth market knowledge to the company. Companies use a varied set of metrics for shortlisting brokers with a proven degree of experience, often evidenced by the broker's track record of selection by clients or by the level of transaction flow. Larger companies often appoint more than one brokers to build relationships on a day-to-day basis to boost liquidity in their shares by market making.

Table : To whom does the IRO report?

Market Cap Strategy	CEO	CFO/CEO	Treasurer
Mega	8%	3%	11%
Large	6%	0%	4%
Mid	19%	2%	5%
Small	27%	8%	3%
Micro	42%	0%	2%

Broking Companies are quite resourceful

"Corporate access team in broking houses can arrange quality meetings"

- Saurabh, Head Investor Relations, Biocon

There is no wrong or right here. There is an increasing thought process that broker organized road shows are probably not the most efficient in meeting the right people. The broker's choice of meeting invites may be motivated by several factors like accreditation by the fund house, brokerage offered, interest in the particular company stock etc. However, a good corporate access team in any brokerage will try and get the best meetings possible, keeping the Company in the loop and taking the Company's meeting interests in mind.

In our Company we have always used brokers to organize road shows for us and they have done a good or decent job. We plan to keep using brokers because we see it as an efficient way of getting things organized. Unless the Company has a large team that can take care of such matters, using a broker helps. Having said that, we plan to improve our investor targeting by being better informed by using knowledge databases that are available and taking help of IR support service providers. This could potentially see us setting up meetings in the future, independent of the broker. We probably will still use brokers for some road shows.

Generally, when doing road shows abroad, especially in UK or US, it is better to use an international broking house. They will have a deeper understanding, relationships, specialist sales and wherewithal to host senior management in the local market as compared to domestic brokers who may have presence there, but not enough influence.

"So what if I am behind bars? My share price too will bounce back once I am out."

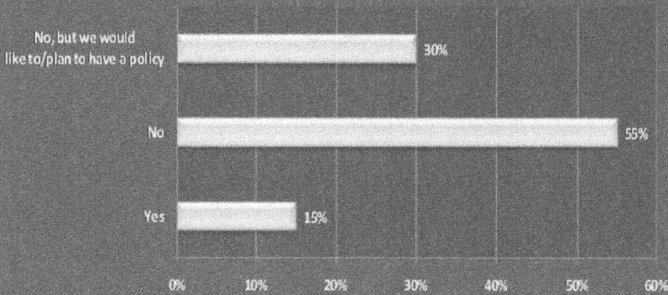

Does your company publish a corporate social responsibility report?

No, but we would like to/plan to have a policy — 30%

No — 55%

Yes — 15%

IR Consultancies

Although a majority of the BSE-Sensex or Nifty 50 companies have dedicated investor relations professionals, other companies may not be able to have a dedicated resource exclusively for this function and hence the CFO, company secretary, and corporate communication, may apportion this activity among themselves. Even with a dedicated IR resource, there could be a need for hiring an external IR consultancy firm for improving reach to investors.

These IR Consultancy firms may help companies by providing:

* All round support to network with analysts and funds on a retained basis.

* Advice and support on share register analysis and on mergers and acquisitions. An effective analysis of the share register will indicate buyers and sellers of the shares; overweight and underweight positions; geographic location; investment style; market and sector weightings; funds under management; and non-holders. This is then benchmarked against the peer group and build proper strategy to do investor targeting.

* With a high probability of investing in the stock to meet with company management.

* Written communicating materials such as website content, investor updates, inputs for annual reports, presentations and other documents.

* Perception studies: there must be a satisfactory dialogue with shareholders based on the mutual understanding of objectives as per corporate governance norms. Hence many companies undertake Perception Studies to ascertain cognition and perception of their stock.

The External IR consultancies can support companies by interviewing a cross section of overweight, underweight and absentee investors to gauge investors' perception and offer effective solutions.

* Road shows: Assist companies in the targeting and organizing road shows due to the intelligence provided by their shareholder analysis and contact relationship management capabilities. By including even the private client stockbroker market, apart from the large institutions, the IR strategy can offer access to a pool of loyal and long-term shareholders.

* Coordination with Financial PR agencies and CEO & Director Finance: Since the corporate reputation and that of its management team are basic influencers of perceptions towards the business as a traded stock, what is to be communicated becomes extremely crucial especially during the IPO, M&A activity, hostile bids, crisis communications, fund-raising or share placing.

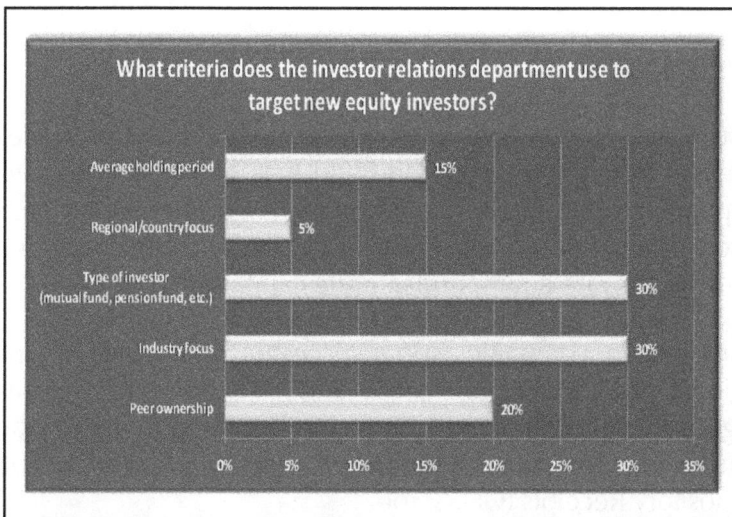

What criteria does the investor relations department use to target new equity investors?

Criteria	Percentage
Average holding period	15%
Regional/country focus	5%
Type of investor (mutual fund, pension fund, etc.)	30%
Industry focus	30%
Peer ownership	20%

Building the IR Program

SWOT Analysis

First of all, a SWOT Analysis of the company's business model is essential to target the right kind and type of investors required. Depending upon the size and complexity of the market sector, a company could choose to attract institutional investors, retail investors, private equity, and venture capitalists.

Many Indian companies were successful in moving up from regional stock exchanges to BSE and NSE. Some of them also hogged the limelight by getting themselves listed in international bourses via American Depository Receipts (ADRs) and Global Depository Receipts (GDRs) too.

Some companies, depending on their commitment to corporate governance and corporate social responsibility also work closely with ethical-oriented and pension funds because these funds also have a great amount of confidence on the company's management, hence,0 they are in a position to commit their investments for a longer period of time.

Some of the factors in an investment proposition include: strong fundamentals for the core business; growth markets; high visibility of future revenues; and debt component. Besides the most important thing is management's philosophy.

Yet another aspect that appeals to investors seeking regular income is on dividend payout policy. Companies which regularly pay dividend are fancied and respected lot when compared to others which don't.

Regular meetings with investors are must to convey your equity story. The company must be well prepared with strong collaterals to ensure meetings are effective. There are a number of regulatory financial calendar requirements which provide great opportunities for the Board to meet the investors throughout the year.

"Dad if I am suffering for any corporate frauds you committed please confess."

Awareness of Regulatory framework is must

"IR Professionals must be aware of Regulatory framework"

**- Poornima Reddy, Company Secretary,
J Kumar Infraprojects**

Awareness of basic regulations is a mandatory aspect even for an IR Professional even though he can always seek an opinion from his company secretary colleague. Following aspects have significance on the IR front:

On time taken by companies to release annual reports after end of the financial year:

As per the listing agreement with the stock exchange, the listed companies have time to conduct AGMs till September 30 and release notice and AR at least 21 days prior to AGM.

On average time taken by companies for releasing their quarterly results:

As per the listing agreement with the stock exchange, a listed company is required to disclose its quarterly earnings within 45 days from close of quarter.

On procedure followed by companies for releasing quarterly results:

After getting the results adopted by the Audit Committee, the results are recommended to the Board which will approve subject to the limited review by the Auditors. Following this, the earnings / disclosures are sent to the stock exchanges. A press release (or a press conference) is given out. The Company may even go for press and TV interviews if there are some major developments to be announced.

On companies conducting analyst meets:

It's not mandatory for listed companies to conduct analyst meets. However, those companies that adopt good corporate governance do practice the procedure to hold analyst meets periodically.

On kind of content required on quarterly presentation slides:

Companies that practice good corporate governance provide significant data, analysis points as part of their quarterly earnings disclosure. This information is readily segmented and provides for an instant overview of the company's financials and performance helping the analysts to take an informed view on the company. Companies which can foresee the future business operations release guidance notes also.

On making selective disclosures:

With several guidelines on corporate governance and accountability in force, companies have put in place several internal procedures to ensure that critical information is handled appropriately and disclosures to the external world do not happen on a selective basis.

On providing guidance:

So companies nowadays provide a road map of their growth plans to investors and analysts on a broad level. This in a way forms as an inclusive strategy and helps the company refine its plans based on the feedback it receives. Companies which can foresee the future business operations release guidance notes also.

On providing presentations on their websites:

Companies do post their quarterly financial presentations and presentations on their website.

On queries raised by analysts and investors during conference calls or analyst meets:

The clarifications sought by analysts during conference calls or meetings are required to be addressed in the quickest possible time.

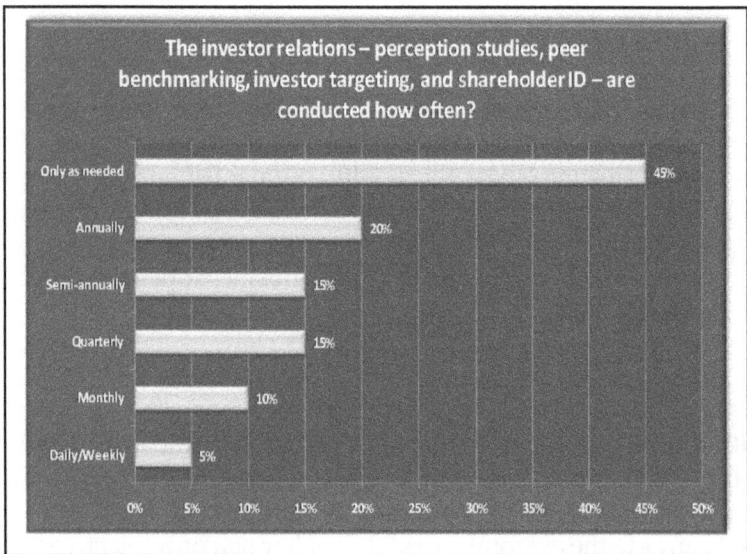

The investor relations – perception studies, peer benchmarking, investor targeting, and shareholder ID – are conducted how often?

Category	Percentage
Only as needed	45%
Annually	20%
Semi-annually	15%
Quarterly	15%
Monthly	10%
Daily/Weekly	5%

Back to Basics...

A Red herring prospectus is an offer document where the price at which the issue is being made and the number of shares is not mentioned as in a book building process.

Site visits

If your operations have a visual element to them, a site visit is a powerful way to convey your story and to give visitors greater insight into the company. Inviting the media, analysts and investors to visit your company will increase their understanding of what you do and how you operate. This also gives an opportunity for them to speak with other employees, and to gauge the quality of the middle management. Events such as the opening of new facilities are the ideal opportunities to host a visit.

Target Messaging to Fund Managers

The message to fund managers is to keep it simple. The better a fund manager understands your business, the more support your company is likely to have in the market. Too many companies feel they have to over promise and then stretch to try and make the numbers. Companies must not resort to a succession of company announcements to sustain the share price. Fund management is a worldwide business with thousands of eyes keeping a look out for opportunities. If you keep producing attractive profit growth then someone will find you and when they do they will want a clear and concise message.

Preparation

It is important that the management is well prepared before any of these meetings, and know what the investor, analyst or journalist is looking for. They must also go through their recent set of reports to know their thought process.

Transparency

In order to maintain fair and transparent markets, it is of fundamental importance that companies keep investors regularly informed about their affairs. The various provisions set relating to company announcements help to create such transparency.

What to announce

The need to provide investors with regular news flow means that companies will need to have in place an annual reporting calendar to enable them to announce certain planned events throughout the year, such as the publication of annual and half-yearly reports.

This apart, companies may hold regular investor briefings and will also communicate with their shareholders at the Annual General Meeting. The periodic publication of news helps to create a balanced and orderly market in a company's securities. However, the ad hoc developments must also be disclosed to the market without delay.

When to announce

Once a company decides that there is inside information, the general rule is to disclose this to the market without delay as there is no reason to delay disclosure either due to a lack of formal Board approval or in order to arrange a parallel event, such as an associated webcast. The practice of delaying an announcement until the formal regulatory information channels are closed is also unacceptable.

If an unexpected significant event occurs about which the company needs more information to make a meaningful announcement, a short delay is acceptable. However, if there is danger of a leak of such information, the company should put out a holding announcement while the issue is investigated. Failure to make such a holding announcement may result in the company's trading being suspended. Among the exceptions are the cases where a company can delay disclosure if its reason for doing so is so as not to prejudice its legitimate interests, provided that: a) such non-disclosure would not be likely to mislead the public; b)any person receiving the information owes the company a duty of confidentiality; and c) the company is able to ensure the confidentiality of that information.

How to announce

The concept of selective disclosure must be done away with and in order to ensure that the information is available to all, an announcement must be done through regulatory channels only.

Annual Report

Due to its statutory nature, the production of the annual report should be seen as a key activity in any company's investor relations program. The annual report is a direct extension of a one-on-one meeting with investors – it gives the strategic detail of the results information. Along with key announcements, the publication date of the annual report should be set well in advance as part of a company's financial calendar.

Many companies view the annual report as the document that brings together all of their key messages throughout the year. It is, in that regard, a sort of 'convenience publishing tool for investors'. It should bring together a description of the business; the context in which the business is operating; an overview of strategy, performance and operations; plus key governance information, including risks and uncertainties. Last, but certainly not least, it should present the main financials, together with detailed explanatory notes.

The Annual Report must give an in-depth understanding of the company, its performance and, crucially, its prospects going forward. Companies which make forward-looking statements focus on their future plans and also use externally-sourced statistics to support their statements for example on growth statistics and the way forward of their own industry vertical.

Management Discussion & Analysis is in vogue

"MDA shows how progressive companies are."

- Ajay Seth, CFO, Maruti Suzuki India

A Management Discussion & Analysis (MDA) is in vogue and is considered as a Best Practice by IR Standards. One can get to see MDA in Annual Reports among few front runners particularly in private sector companies. Many companies fall under the category of "also ran" and make it a point to devote about half a page and comprehensive to give an overview on the current economy, impact on industry and company's business. Besides giving a gist of factors affecting the past performance, it should also provide outlook for the business. A good MDA should also focus on key risks faced by the business along with risk mitigation plan. From providing the gist of financials to operations, sustainability to market outlook, the MDA should give the comprehensive assessment of the management about the business to help investors to take decisions.

The Annual Report of the company is a key information document for all the stakeholders. The companies with better IR practices should form MDA as a part of the Annual Report, thereby adding value to the annual report.

MDA Structure:

A Management Discussion & Analysis may include discussion on the following matters within the limits set by the company's competitive position:

i.   Industry structure and developments.
ii.   Opportunities and Threats.
iii. Segment–wise or product-wise performance.
iv.   Outlook
v.   Risks and concerns.
vi.   Internal control systems and their adequacy.
vii. Discussion on financial performance with respect to operational performance.
Viii. Material developments in Human Resources / Industrial Relations front, including number of people employed.

Design: Some companies nowadays hire the services of annual report design and consultancy specialists to help them structure and design the content – print and online -the look and feel should be specifically designed with maze of information included within the report. It must be remembered that the audiences will access the information in different ways. Some would like to read the content in depth, but many will be looking for a quick read approach, hence, pulling out key messages and content is crucial.

Recently, a range of online formats have emerged. Many listed companies make their annual reports available as a PDF online – thereby satisfying the need to produce the same content in print and online. Some Large-Cap companies also produce annual reports as full web pages. Others have opted to produce the front 'narrative sections' of their reports in HTML, while keeping the back section as PDFs. Companies must think about the needs of their audiences while also considering a range of other factors, such as budget, accessibility and transition towards wider online communications. The annual report forms a part of wider online investor communi cations effort and sits comfortably alongside

electronic versions of investor presentations, share price charts and AGM information.

The obligations of companies to provide timely disclosure of price sensitive information have always been central to the regulatory regime. However, with the advent of the internet, a practical shift in disclosures too has been noticed. The websites are the first touch point between an investor and a company and so act as a standard-bearer for the corporate brand and values. As standards improved so have the expectations on the quality of the website. Some investors also judge management's perception on investors through the quality of their website.

For companies who are making the transition from private to public ownership through an IPO, the website is particularly important. You may have more people looking at your site over the course of two weeks than you will for the next two years. Since in the run up to an IPO, the demands on the senior management's time will be enormous, it pays to think about it early and get a good framework of corporate information in place long before any announcements are made.

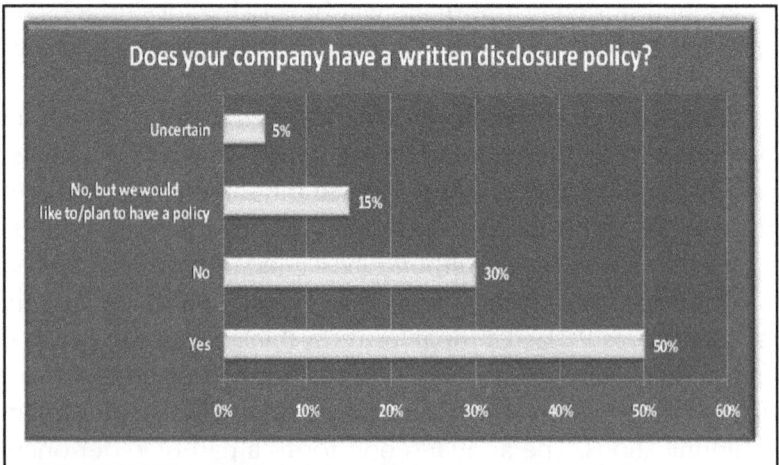

Does your company have a written disclosure policy?

Response	Percentage
Uncertain	5%
No, but we would like to/plan to have a policy	15%
No	30%
Yes	50%

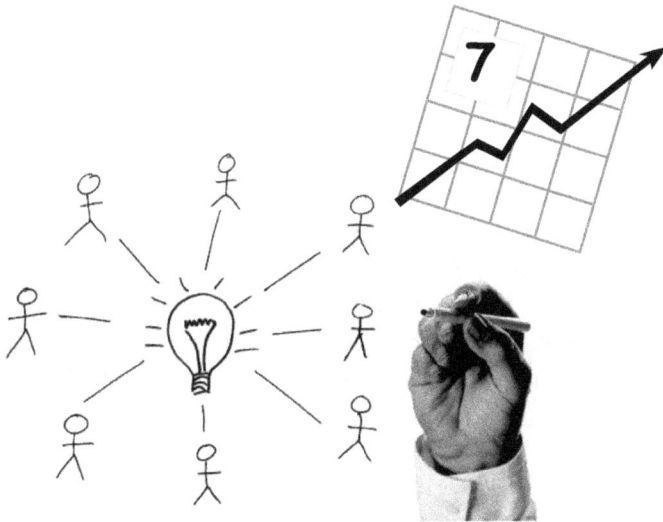

IR in Practice

IR is probably one of the most exciting professions seated at the heart of the company, as it is an integral part of the corporate strategy to seek better valuations and gain visibility in the market place. Some of the day-to-day IR activities include:

Telephone support:

For analysts, the IRP will be the first point of call. On a daily basis, it is the IRP who deals with the analysts. Occasionally others like the CFO or the CEO shall pitch in to interact with the analysts if the company is passing through very exciting times. A telephone call, though it appears to be informal, is actually not. The same

rules and regulations shall apply to telephone conversations as in the case of any other form of communication. Hence, only the information available in the public domain needs to be share with the analysts.

A proactive IRP generally calls up the analysts, following an announcement, to check that they have a good understanding of the message. This proactive gesture by the IRP shall help in avoiding any errors if any. This way, if companies are able to position themselves as being proactive, phone conversations tend to become the main vehicle for exchanging information. This mode shall enable the companies to gather a lot of vital information in their industry which shall empower them to know their ranking vis-à-vis their competitors in various segments.

One-on-ones:

An IRP must know well in advance as to who can get greater mileage for his company. Accordingly, he must have the profile of various analysts (both on the sell-side as well as on the buy-side), their ratings on the peer group, the frequency with which they shuffle their portfolio, their investment style, the size of their fund, and other such vital information.

Based on the above information, the IRP must filter the requests made by various analysts (for one-on-ones) so that he can accordingly brief the management and save it's valuable time It is therefore essential that an IRP has sound knowledge of his company's share register. A few issues that need to be considered prior to scheduling a meeting shall include:

- Why is the institution keen on meeting? What could be areas of its interests?
- Do they hold any shares in the company?
- If so, how much? And, were there any recent changes in their holdings?

- If not, do they hold in the peer group? And, are they likely to invest?
- Have they met the management before? If so, have they acquired any shares after the meeting?
- How do they perceive the company's management?

Road shows:

A crucial factor required for the success of road shows is effective targeting of institutional players in order to save precious time of the company's management. Quite often, a few sell-side brokers may offer to organize road shows on behalf of the company.

These brokers have specialist sales people located in various countries with excellent contacts and local knowledge. Nevertheless it is important though, to keep overall management of the roads how in-house because the company alone will know its share register better than anyone else.

For conducting well-planned road shows, an IRP takes the following steps:

- Block management time in diaries early
- Decide which institutions/countries to target
- Discuss target list with advisers and make appropriate amendments.
- Maintain record of institutions who refuse to attend road shows.
- Undertake perception audit.
- Give proper feedback to management.

Seminars and Conferences:

This mechanism provides a proper platform for the key audiences to keep themselves updated and network with operational directors who normally they would have little exposure to. Events like these provide a good environment for informal networking.

An IRP may have to deal with the following issues:

- What ought to be the theme of the seminar?
- Who is going speak on which subject?
- Have right kind of audience.
- Freeze a date that does not clash with any other sector or important market events.
- Make sure of directors' availability.
- Must give the same amount of importance to the event as one normally gives to the financial results.
- If any price sensitive information is disclosed at the event, it has to be ensured that the same is disseminated in the form of news release.
- Ensure a simultaneous disclosure by means of web or audio-casting.

Company Meetings

On their own companies can set up meetings and invite the targeted audience like the analysts, portfolio managers, and other institutional shareholders. Despite holding huge seminars and meetings, many companies default if they fail to share any important information. It has to be remembered that none of the investors are generally interested in historical information or a lengthy technical description of their products.

Investors crave insightful discussion on the company's strategic direction and its major initiatives. Discussion on the company's strengths and opportunities and how has it positioned itself against competition would generally evoke interest in investors' community for they would look forward to the company's willingness to share information on various challenges confronting the company. A company's management which is bubbling with confidence and is in total command of what is happening across its industry often gets mileage in the investors' community.

Management must be involved in Investor Conferences

"Senior Management presence at Investors Conference is important."

- Ananth Kumar, Director, Oil India

Involvement of several members of the senior management at investor conferences to provide a broader mosaic of information to investors and illustrate the depth of the management is generally well received by investors.

At least about 10 members of our senior management, including our business group leaders, are available to go out on the road and meet with investors. Investors appreciate meeting with business unit heads who are close to our customers and have profit & loss responsibility. Meeting with investors also helps our senior management team better understand how investors make buy/hold/sell decisions on our stock.

Senior management is also expected to devote adequate time for Investor Relations function. The investment community expects direct access to the senior management. Senior management must spend time, be present and also be involved at meetings with large institutional investors. This apart, seniors are expected to be present during the presentations at investor conferences, and quarterly results conference calls.

Quality time from senior management is one of the most important aspects of investor meetings. This is also best evaluated during the one-on-one meetings. Hence, senior management sets- aside adequate time to meet up with the investors.

Further it is the general expectation that the senior management must attend and participate in at least two investor conferences in India and one investor conference abroad, based on the need. It's also generally agreed that seniors need to try meeting institutional investors on a one-on-one basis if not to attend a non-deal road show organized by sell-side houses.

"Today CEO is foul mood, we must jack up the share price to please him"

Back to Basics...

In a book-built issue, the price at which the shares will be allotted and the successful allottees will be decided upon by a bidding process. The process of bidding will be done as per the rules laid down by SEBI.

Plant Visits

Plant visits shall enable to add more spice to otherwise routine formal financial meetings and presentations. Over here, an IRP must ensure that the employees on-site are having a fair amount of idea as to what constitutes price-sensitive information. Enough care and precautions must be taken to ensure that the safety regulations and logistics run smoothly.

Group Meetings

Meetings like these provide an opportunity to meet up with the senior management on a one-on-one basis. Some small investors who feel that they are not sufficiently informed about the company's activities prefer such a route. These days, such meetings are becoming increasingly popular and they are called as "reverse road-shows". To such meetings, the broker brings in a fund manager or a group of investors and arranges a series of meetings on their behalf.

IR Website/Investors Link

The Investor Relations website or the Investors Link on the company's website increasingly attracts the analysts, both from the buy-side as well as the sell-side, for quick browsing on the company's financials. Vital information of the likes of, real-time stock prices, trading volume, historical prices, earnings, event calendar pertaining to the financial results and board meetings, analysts tracking the company and their ratings, and corporate profile, are generally included in the Investors' Link. Since maintaining such vital information on the site is a non-core function for any company, a few firms are outsourcing this work of maintenance. Interestingly, the moment an investor clicks on the Investors' Link, it gets connected to the firm's server where data is maintained and constantly updated.

E-Mail Exchange

E-mail is catching up fancy among the analysts community for quick dissemination of information. The IRPs maintain a database of all those analysts who matter both on the buy-side as well as on the sell-side. For an IRP, e-mail also offers a few other advantages since the e-mail identifies investors and also offers a total count of the investors sending the queries. This also helps the company to know which analysts actively track the company and are hungry for data. On the domestic front, Infosys offers a wide variety of company information online to investors. Its Investors' Relations Link on the Website provides investors with current reports on its earnings, annual reports for last few years, share price movement and volume of trades, its historical stock pricing, and other media releases.

Crisis Management

Crises are inevitable, hence it is essential to be prepared to deal with them:

Step 1: An Early Warning System

By undertaking Perception Audit, it is possible to know how the company is perceived in the community of analysts, customers, suppliers, business leaders, industry associations, regulators, and its own employees. Excellent contacts with people like these shall help the company to pick up rumors and also more importantly, help to trace the source of such rumors.

Step 2: Put Together a Crisis Team

The so-called Crisis Team shall include representatives from different divisions of the likes of, finance, marketing, operations, manufacturing, corporate communications, human resources, regulatory affairs, and investor relations.

Step 3: Determining the Message and Information

In the event of crisis, it is to be ensured whether this would affect the company's core story and facts. Hence, while the events unfold, a careful thinking up front, based on the best information available is required. Better still would be to always send a written communication to the markets since it enables the company to be more articulate and precise in presenting information.

"We have come up this far, thanks to markets, sustaining this trend is becoming difficult..."

IR is not mere number crunching

"IR Professionals must possess several soft skills and it's not a just number crunching job"

- Shalender Maru, IR Head, Edelweiss

SOFT SKILLS too matter a great deal, and IR is not a mere number-crunching job. The following soft-skills are very important in an IR function:

- Providing Honest, Timely and Accurate business information.
- Proactive Communication.
- Maintaining Transparency.
- Awareness about company's current and future events.
- Building Rapport, Trust and Confidence among investors and analysts.
- Continuous Interaction with analysts and investors regarding business events & updates.
- Attracting new and retaining current investors.
- Promoting the company to both investors as well as analysts.
- Analyzing Research Reports, Earning Estimates and keeping track of competitors.
- Conducting one-on-one meetings on a regular basis.
- Organizing Road Shows.

- Conducting Quarterly Earning Call for investors and analysts with the management.
- Organizing Site Visits
- Attending Conferences of sell-side analyst.
- Providing senior management with regular feedback from the market.
- Keeping the management informed about the latest happenings in the market.
- Compiling a summary of competitors' earnings reports, and forwarding key economic data.
- Analyzing and updating the management about stock performance of the company v/s peers.
- Alerting the management team to any unusual or increased trading activity.
- Setting up management meetings with investors and analysts.

Does the investor relations department have a written crisis communications policy?

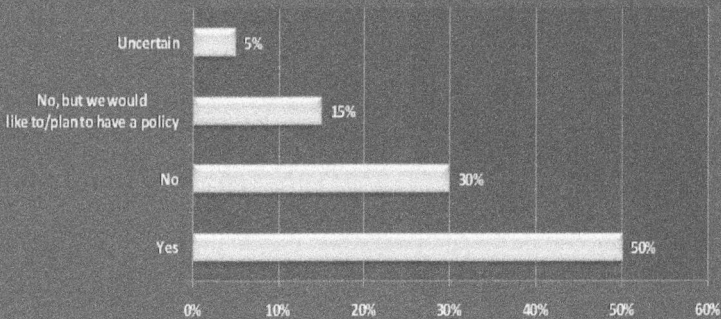

Response	Percentage
Uncertain	5%
No, but we would like to/plan to have a policy	15%
No	30%
Yes	50%

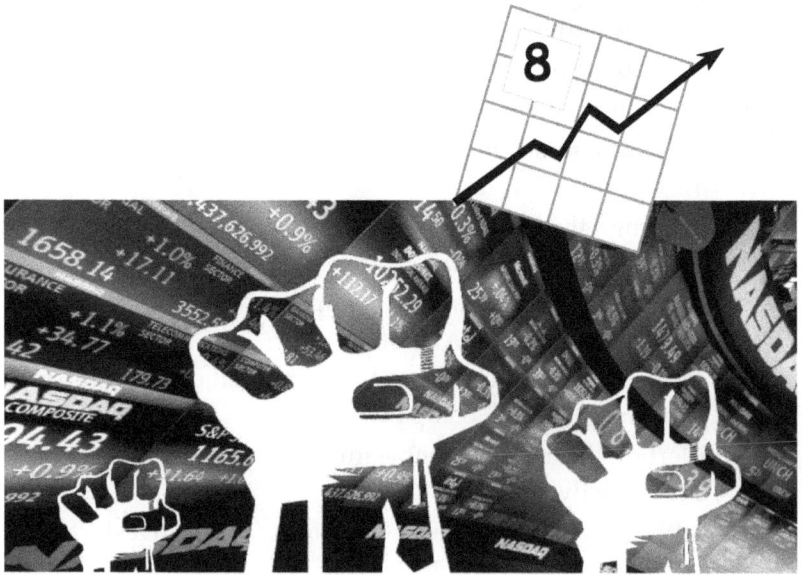

Shareholders' Activism

Shareholders' activism catching up in India

"What Gets Measured, Gets Done,"

- Amit Tandon, MD, IIAS

We wanted Investors again, hence we decided to raise funds yet again!

"What an excuse to meet us!!!"

Institutional EYE

The new Clause 49 and Clause 35B will play a large role in strengthening the corporate governance landscape in India. Last year, SEBI began consultations with market participants in order to revise and overhaul the corporate governance norms for listed companies. With the recent notification of the relevant sections of the Act (which come into effect from 1 April 2014), SEBI released the revised clauses 35B and 49 of the Listing Agreement. "SEBI's new Clause 49 uses disclosure as an enforcement tool: publicly disseminating information will create comparability, thereby fostering an environment of competitive behavior that serves shareholders and the corporate governance agenda," says Amit Tandon, Managing Director, Institutional Investor Advisory Services (IIAS).

These guidelines require greater disclosures on the performance and review of the board of directors. Companies are now required to disclose, in their Annual Reports, granular details on director compensation (including ESOPs), directors' performance evaluation metrics, directors' training, the board's code of conduct and compliance with it, a resume of directors to be appointed, and the directors' resignation letters. IIAS believes that the enforced transparency in the operations of the board will compel it to be more mindful of its role. Simultaneously, reputation risks of greater disclosures will induce companies to follow more stringent norms while selecting members of the board, its ultimate oversight body (refer Annexure A).

SEBI has also used internal disclosure mechanisms effectively to curb promoters' powers. The crux of strong internal controls lies in the independence and objectivity of the internal administrators. Therefore, SEBI has tightened the definition of independent directors and then provided them with stronger oversight. All related party transactions will be approved by the Audit Committee of which at least 2/3rd will comprise independent directors. The new guidelines require an independent director on the board of the listed company to also be on the board of its unlisted subsidiary. The Audit Committee of the listed company will review the financial statements of its unlisted subsidiaries, and the minutes of board meetings of material unlisted subsidiaries will now need to be presented to the board of the parent company. These measures reign in the hitherto unlimited powers that promoters enjoyed over unlisted subsidiaries.

The new guidelines align the provisions of the Listing Agreement with those of the Companies Act 2013 and at places, have gone beyond this (refer Annexure B).While the new norms may appear onerous to companies, IIAS believes that these establish the much needed corporate governance framework in today's context.

Annexure A: Disclosures Required

Accounting Treatment:

- In cases where there is a deviation from the general Accounting Standards the management's explanation as to why it believes such alternative treatment is more representative should be disclosed

Board Appointments:

- The letter of appointment along with the detailed profile of the independent director shall be disclosed on the websites of the company and the Stock Exchanges.
- The company shall disclose the criteria for performance evaluation, as laid down by the Nomination Committee, in its Annual Report.
- The details of training imparted to directors shall be disclosed in the Annual Report
- The details of establishment of whistle-blower policy shall be disclosed by the company on its website and in the Board's report.

- The evaluation criteria for appointment of directors to be disclosed.
- The Code of Conduct for the Board of Directors and the senior management shall be disclosed on the website of the company.
- The company shall disclose the letter of resignation along with the detailed reasons of resignation provided by the director of the company on its website.
- Non-executive directors shall disclose their shareholding in the listed company in which they are proposed to be appointed as directors, prior to their appointment.
- The mandate, composition and working procedures of each board committee should be well defined and disclosed.

Restructuring/Related Party Transactions

- The company shall formulate a policy for determining 'material' subsidiaries and such policy shall be disclosed to Stock Exchanges and in the Annual Report.
- The company shall disclose the policy on dealing with Related Party Transactions on its website and also in the Annual Report.
- Details of all material transactions with related parties shall be disclosed quarterly along with the compliance report on corporate governance.
- Senior management shall make disclosures to the board relating to all material transactions, where they have personal interest, that may have a potential conflict with the interest of the company at large.

Remuneration

- All pecuniary relationships or transactions of the non-executive directors vis-à-vis the company shall be disclosed in the Annual Report.
- Remuneration policy for directors has to be disclosed.

- Details of fixed component and performance linked incentives, along with the performance criteria to be disclosed.
- Stock option details, if any - and whether issued at a discount as well as the period over which accrued and over which exercisable has to be disclosed.
- The company shall publish its criteria of making payments to non-executive directors in its annual report.
- The company shall disclose the number of shares and convertible instruments held by non-executive directors in the annual report.

"I am trying to sing a different tune to investors this time around..."

Back to Basics...

The Green Shoe Option is used by companies making an issue to stabilize the price in the secondary markets.